eBooks:

How to Sell & Market Them

by

Darin Jewell &

Conrad Jones

Author Credentials

Darin Jewell

Darin Jewell is Managing Director of The Inspira Group Literary Agency. He published *How to Sell & Market Your Book* in 2010 which tells authors how to raise their literary profile and promote their books in easy and effective ways. It sets out the resources available and outlines which paths are likely to sell the most copies and which will establish the writer as a published author, and as a marketable and commercial brand.

As Director of a professional literary agency, he receives hundreds of requests for representation from authors each month and regularly participates as a panelist in Writing Seminars and speaks to various Writing Groups each year. He advises authors on how they can drive and manage each stage of the publishing process for their books from production to pricing right through to promotion.

Darin has placed over a hundred books in the last decade with traditional publishers and represents Michael G. R. Tolkien, Kevin Joslin, David Barry, best-selling business book author Fergus O'Connell, best-selling humor writer Mark Leigh, best-selling eBook author Conrad Jones and Mind, Body, Spirit (MBS) author Simon Brown whose *Feng Shui* book has sold over a million copies to date.

Conrad Jones

Conrad started writing as a business venture. It was a change of career, not an artistic project. Although he eventually achieved a respectable income from his books, things were not simple in the beginning and he learned some harsh lessons along the way. Based on his varied experiences in selling and promoting his own eBooks, Conrad explains to authors the things that worked and the things that didn't. He had no agent to start and no publisher to guide and support his efforts. Rather, he learned the hard way, through trial and error.

It was a back-to-front journey but the success of his eBook sales earned him the interest of a good agent and a publishing deal. If you can follow the simple guidelines and tips set out in this book then you can build sales and prove to the traditional industry that you are a saleable asset in the literary world. Or, if you prefer, you can choose to go it alone and still make a decent residual monthly income.

When Conrad turned his paperbacks into eBooks, his thriller series stormed the Kindle charts. Within 3 weeks of launching them, he had two titles (*The Child Taker* and *Slow Burn*) in the top ten Kindle lists. Not genre lists, the overall sales chart. All seven of his thrillers were in the top 40 for nearly 12 months. On the release of his 8th book (*Nine Angels*), it flew to number 3 in the horror charts overnight. *The Child Taker* was number 1 in thriller law books and Tank was number 1 in thriller war books. He achieved over 120,000 digital downloads in the first year. It wasn't just luck. Rather, it was the success of building a marketing base over a period of years and then applying everything that he had learned to the launch of his eBooks. His credentials are actual book sales, a growing fan base and over 250 five-star reviews across the *Soft Target* series.

This book is dedicated to

Aidan Jewell and Aimee Jewell

Contents

Chapter 1

Setting Realistic Sales Targets

Most of the tips and process in this guide are used on a daily basis by successful authors and publishers. Because of the internet, we are in a position to reach and touch millions of readers across the globe and if you can grasp the basics and use them regularly then you will sell your books. Marketing is a relentless but essential part of publishing. To be successful, you need to set aside time every working day to update your profile, assess reviews, social network and monitor sales and promotions.

To set sales targets and plan a marketing strategy it is useful to know how established brands achieve this. Take, for example, an Area Manager for McDonalds Restaurants. Each restaurant is held accountable for its sales increases or decreases on a daily, weekly, monthly and yearly basis. This constant monitoring of each individual restaurant's growth and profitability is integral to their success. As a store manager, you are encouraged to market your restaurant locally, and amazingly simple ideas can actually turn declining restaurants into goldmines. McDonalds is one of the most successful and recognizable brands on the planet and you can emulate them by working on a daily basis to raise your literary profile and build up your author name as a recognised brand. It's as easy as PIE. Plan, Implement and Evaluate.

As an author without the backing of a big publisher, book marketing is your number one priority but many authors find that sitting down and planning a marketing campaign is alien to them. I am not going to tell you that it is easy because it isn't but if you follow the core basics, you will develop your marketing skills alongside your writing.

You have to dedicate as much time and effort into selling your book as you did writing it. To make it more approachable, let's break it down into areas we can look at individually. You have to separate them to plan them effectively. Once we have looked at the basics of marketing, you should have a complete overview of what's involved in successfully marketing your book and allowing it to reach its full potential, without breaking the bank. Some of the eBook marketing tips in this book are case specific but they may provoke ideas which you can adapt to your circumstances.

It's important that we're realistic about potential sales that can be reasonably achieved, that we set challenging but achievable targets. Every reader has their favorite authors and genres. Few James Herbert fans will have rushed out to buy *Fifty Shades of Grey*. If your book has a potential readership then finding them and letting them know that your book is available is the key to selling it. Once it is selling, your readers will soon let you know if it is any good or not!

The most important element in book marketing is not how much money you have to throw at a promotional campaign; it is the drive and commitment of the individual author and the commercial potential of the book itself. If your book is full of dross, then it simply won't sell. If it's about thermonuclear-physics in the bathroom or it is a collection of poems that have special meaning to you, then your market is limited. That doesn't mean no one will buy it, just be realistic about sales projections.

The majority of self-published print-on-demand books sell less than 200 copies. Of course, there have been exceptions but that is your first goal. Beat the average and you have succeeded. If your book is good, then you will beat that sales figure in your first campaign. There are several different measures of what constitutes a bestseller. In the main, 10,000 copies in the first 12 months or 15,000 in total can be classed as bestsellers while other gurus have moved the yard-stick to 35,000 copies. The point that I want to make is that these are largely variable figures and success is relative to the format, pricing and promotional support.

Chapter 2

There is no marketing substitute for a good eBook

Why do some eBooks sell well on the internet while others flounder? Sometimes it is simply timing but mostly it is the quality of the product which drives sales through word of mouth or "viral" marketing. There are literally thousands of great storylines and plots that have floundered because the editing and proofreading isn't up to scratch. You should do all that you can to avoid writing defects into your book, because a book that is poorly edited, hard to read or difficult to position within the market is going to meet significant obstacles finding a wide readership.

Make sure your book conforms to generally-accepted editing and design standards so you don't cripple your own marketing efforts. Do not rely on one set of eyes to proof your novel, especially your own. You will only read what you think you have written.

Quality books will give you a return on your marketing investment because once other people learn about the product, they are much more likely to buy it and recommend it to others. Endorsements and positive reviews from your readers is the biggest seller of books. Look at *Neuromancer* by William Gibson which came from a little-known author as his debut book to sell millions of copies and win the science-fiction "triple crown" — the Nebula Award, the Philip K. Dick Award, and the Hugo Award.

How many times did avid sci-fi readers recommend this book on specialist fantasy and sci-fi discussion boards, in sci-fi ezines and on Goodreads and Lovereading websites, and why did their reviews make such an impact in the book charts?

Similarly, why has *The Da Vinci Code* sold in excess of 80 million copies worldwide? The reason is clear. Dan Brown insinuated that Jesus had a living bloodline and that the Virgin was buried beneath the inverted pyramid at the Louvre. That got tongues wagging! The fiction was so cleverly entwined in the facts that many people believed the hype and had to read it for themselves.

Fifty Shades of Grey is hot and steamy and it had women intrigued as to how pornographic it really was, but the key to all three of these books in different genres is that people raved about them to other people. There's nothing like a good endorsement or review to help sell your book, and good recommendations come from well-written and professionally edited books.

Why mention these books in particular? Because all three of these books were in print and available for a while before they took off. Word-of-mouth or "viral marketing" as it is commonly referred to within literary circles, and word-of-mouse or "social networking" as it is commonly known, launched these novels because they were appealing and once people started talking about them online and offline, they sold millions.

There are many reasons why different kinds of books sell, and we can identify a few clear reasons why some sell better than others:

- It is unique and has current information that's in demand, but that cannot be found anywhere else

- It has a story which is compelling and entertaining

- The author is a well-known celebrity or a well-established author with a large following

- The book sells well and as sales grow, people start talking about it and telling others about the book

I am guessing not many celebrities or their ghost-writers are going to buy this book so I'll rule that one out for now. Only you and the readers can decide if your story is compelling and entertaining so your goal is get people talking about you and your book.

This last point is the ultimate goal of our marketing efforts. No one will raise a huge flag and launch fireworks for you when you upload your book and you cannot force people to buy it, no matter how much money you spend on advertising or how many times you appear in the newspapers or on radio shows. They have no longevity. Influencing people in an endearing manner is the key to gaining interest over a prolonged period. A friend or colleague at work who tells you that you "have to read this book" is a far more powerful marketing tool than any other.

You have to begin building a brand from day one and this book explains how to make people remember you as well as your books. You want every reader you meet to hear about your book and to tell their friends about your story as well as the titles of your other books.

Chapter 3

Building Yourself Up as a Brand Name

You need to market yourself as well as your book, which means communicating the message that you want others to hear about your books to a plethora of audiences over a sustained period of time. You have dedicated time and effort into spreading the word, growing your brand and converting readers into fans who will tell their friends and buy your next book.

Branding is something people hear a lot about but don't fully understand how complex it can be. Examples of good branding are BMW, Microsoft and Virgin. If you buy a product with their brand name on it, you are expecting it to be reliable and great quality. If you shop for beans at Aldi or Lidl, you know the products will be good but perhaps not the same quality as beans from Sainsbury's.

A well-known example of poor branding is when Gerald Ratner, the Chief Executive of the once profitable Ratners Group of jewelers made a speech at the Institute of Directors in London in April 1991, and commented:

"We do cut-glass sherry decanters complete with six glasses on a silver-plated tray that your butler can serve you drinks on, all for £4.95. People say, 'How can you sell this for such a low price?' I say, 'Because it's total crap.'"

He compounded this by going on to remark that some of the earrings were "Cheaper than an M&S prawn sandwich but probably wouldn't last as long."

Ratner's comments are textbook examples of how you can alienate your target market with substandard quality and off-the-cuff remarks. Consumers exacted their revenge by staying away from Ratner shops. The value of Ratners Group plummeted by £500 million, which nearly lead to the company's collapse. Ratner subsequently resigned in November 1992 and the group changed its name to Signet Group in September 1993 because the "Ratner" brand had suffered immeasurably from this marketing faux-pas.

It takes a lot of time and promotional work to establish yourself as an author and a brand name by following the tips set out in this book, but only a few minutes to lose that hard-won credibility and fan base by publishing books that have not been professionally proofread or making caustic remarks on discussion boards or on Amazon (as one best-selling eBook author did recently in criticizing reviewers of his book, leading Amazon to throw him off the site for a period of time, costing him both readers and revenue).

As an author, you cannot separate yourself from your books completely even if you use a pen-name, because you still have to work with people who will be aware of the author's real name. In fact, writing under a pen-name can limit your marketing activities in some ways. Likewise, uploading positive reviews of your book disguised as "anonymous" postings on discussion boards or adding five-star reviews of your book on Amazon can detract rather than enhance your book's marketing reach because it's obvious which glowing, detailed reviews are written by authors, especially those that say "a must-read" and "I cannot wait for the author's next book."

If you criticize your publisher for not doing more, or harass retailers for not stocking your book, then no one will want to work with you and your books won't have a chance. Likewise, if your readers take time to review your book, even negatively, you should consider carefully what they say and respond positively to them. Take care not to take your readers for granted, or you will lose them quicker than you gained them. Listen closely to your readers, and give them what they're asking for.

You and your books are your brand. Your books are your logo and will be your readers' first impression of you, hence it is vital that you get the title and the covers right. Along with the story-lines that you skillfully and painstakingly weave together, your author brand is how you pitch your work and how you conduct yourself.

Good examples of branding in the literary world are Mills and Boon. Everyone knows that they publish romantic novels. Stephen King is a horror and thriller writer that most people will know which is why his name is larger than the title on his last five books. Julia Donaldson is author of over 120 children's books and on the cover of many of them it states boldly "by the Children's Laureate and author of *The Gruffalo*".

I took my children to see Julia Donaldson speak at the Wonderlands Festival of Writing and expected a question-and-answer session with the author talking about herself, her main inspiration for writing best-loved children's stories, and what she's working on next. Instead, she involved most all of the hundred or so children in the audience over the course of an hour and acted out her stories and sang songs accompanied by her multi-talented guitar-playing husband, Malcolm.

J. K. Rowling has set a great example to writers by playing down her success and being pragmatic during interviews. Many people will know that she wrote her early novels in cafes in Edinburgh because the walk there helped get her young daughter to sleep and that she was a single mother at the time. Her brand is her Harry Potter novels first, and her personal "rags to riches" life story has added to her overall brand because she came from humble beginnings and downplays her success.

You are your brand. Get people to like you and they will want to read your books.

Forget about your eBook as the focus for a moment and concentrate on building up yourself as a brand. You may have heard of the term "personal branding." It's a phrase popular with personal development that means "how you present yourself to the world." This obviously applies to the literary and business world and also to your extended circle of contacts. The main idea is that whether you like it or not, the world is going to have an opinion about you which will be manufactured from how you conduct yourself in the public arena. Most people don't think too much about how they're seen by others but if you put yourself out there by sharing your expertise or as a raconteur, telling a story through your book, you will be judged. That is just human nature. As a published author, you can no longer just live and let the world think of you however they'd like.

"Personal branding" is about intentionally influencing how the world sees you by behaving in a certain manner. It's about purposefully packaging that "brand called you," making sure that it is a likable package. The benefits are obvious. The better prepared you are to show the world who you are, the more likely the world will see you the way you want. That means your readers and reviewers. That means interviewers from the press or radio. That means people searching for you and your books online. That means your social circles, family, friends and other professionals from the literary world.

When you have a solid personal brand, you'll be more memorable, you'll be more impressive, and people will end up having a more favorable opinion about you. They will be more likely to go away and look at your product if they like you – that's the same thing that good branding does for a product.

How to Actually Build an Author Brand In Practice

Like most things in the world of "personal development," "personal branding" is a fairly vague concept. It is a great idea in theory but how do you actually sit down and plan how to do it? It's one of those things that sound nice, but discussions about it tend to be impractical or not actionable enough to be useful. If an idea isn't practical is it worth much? The answer is obviously no, so let's be practical and use some basics to develop a plan. Follow these 6 easy steps or adapt them to suit you and you'll have worked out a personal brand you can start using today:

Step 1: Choose the core focus for your personal brand

Every brand is based on a few memorable qualities which marketing people take to focus on. For instance, Ford Motor Company does not market their vehicles on their green credentials or their safety record. They market them on their quality and contemporary styling and up to the minute technology. Focusing on a few key qualities makes it easier to connect and remember the product it's attached to.

Another good example of branding is Apple. Apple sells computers, phones, and software. You could say a lot about them, but their brand is focused. Apple's brand is fun, slick, stylish, cutting-edge, reliable, and virus-free. Their brand is focused and it's positive. You need to do the same. Choose a handful of qualities about yourself that you want to be known for. Maybe you're witty when you write blogs or interact with people, or maybe you are an excellent reviewer of other authors' books. Or maybe you're a confident, detail oriented, serious, leader who's a crazy New York Yankees fan.

What collection of attributes do you want to be known for by the world? Make sure you don't try to focus on too many things – it'll be harder for someone to remember any of it. Concentrate on two key aspects and maybe three or four minor ones. Oh, and make sure you're honest with yourself – pretending to be something you're not never works well and there are many trolls out there who will see through you and take great pleasure in dissecting your mistakes in the public eye.

Start with this: Write down 4 or 5 things you want the world to know about you.

Step 2: Prioritize your core brand focus

It's easier for people remember one thing than several things. It's easier for people to focus on doing one thing than doing a lot of things. For example, most websites want their visitors to do a variety of things – get on an email list, bookmark the site, click on an ad, buy a product, comment, share on social media, etc. The more of those things a website focuses on, the less likely visitors are to do anything but go to a different website. Too many options lead to inaction. The same concept is true for your personal branding. The more you throw at someone, the less likely they are to remember any of it. So what you have to do is look at your list of 4 or 5 qualities about yourself and decide which of them is the most important. If someone could define you by one quality, which would it be? The other things, though important, can be secondary elements in your personal brand.

Rank your 4 or 5 elements by importance to you.

Step 3: Make your elements into priority list

As a general rule, people will talk up the importance of things like personal elevator statements and personal mission statements too much. Even so, the process of developing one helps take something general (like a list of 5 qualities about you) and makes it easier to talk about convincingly. That's important, because it can be hard to talk about something you haven't already thought through.

Have you ever talked about something in public without first having time to think about what you had to say? For example, has someone ever asked you to tell a story about something funny that happened to you? You remembered exactly what happened, but just never thought through how to tell it. So you try to tell your story, but your audience's eyes glaze over because you're not telling it well, and you eventually end awkwardly with, "Oh, well, I guess you had to have been there for it to be funny."

It's a similar situation with your personal brand. You need to think through how to communicate it or it won't be useful.

Here's the best way to work through that quickly:

1) Pull up something that can record audio on your computer or phone.

2) Record yourself talking about each of your 4 to 5 qualities, why they are important, why other people

should think they're important, and examples that would show the world you have them.

3) Ramble on and on until your ideas start solidifying. Talk until it starts feeling more comfortable and natural to talk about them.

4) Once you start feeling comfortable with what you're saying, stop recording, and listen to it.

5) Write down the most compelling things you said – the things you think are the smartest, most eloquent things you said about yourself.

6) Condense the best things you said about yourself into three sentences that emphasize your primary characteristic while including the others. (This is your "elevator pitch" for the purpose of this exercise).

Actually work through this stuff by recording yourself, taking notes, and distilling it into an elevator statement of sorts. Don't stress about getting it perfect. This an exercise in narrowing down the excess so that you have a convincing paragraph of information which will be your core focus. If you practice it, then it will become more convincing.

Step 4: Focus your online identity with your new core statement

Like it or not, what you do online influences how others perceive you and also your product. If you want your personal brand to be effective, your online accounts at Facebook, Twitter, LinkedIn, and your other online profiles need to reflect the ideas in your core statement from Step 3. If you were a stranger looking at your online accounts, would your main takeaway reflect your personal brand? If you look at Conrad Jones' Facebook account or fan page, then you'll recognize he is a thriller writer. He doesn't post what he is having for breakfast but he does post every review that he carries out or receives. If you visit it then you would be under no illusions that he is an author, and the genre that he's writing in.

If your Facebook pages do not do then, then you need to start adjusting things that you have online and take your time to get it right and stick to those key focal points. Don't copy and paste your core statement to your Facebook profile, that would look unprofessional and somewhat retentive. Instead, emphasize the things that make your personal brand stronger online and de-emphasize the things that conflict with it. For example, if you said you're a published author and reviewer, delete that quote about disliking someone's book.

Take a quick audit of your online profiles and start adjusting things so they reflect the elements of your personal brand and concentrate on the core ideals.

Step 5: Take more control of your online brand identity

Most companies have a presence on social media nowadays that reflect their brand. But their online platform is a website they own. The reason for that is simple. You can manage your online profiles, but you have complete control over a website you own. The same is true for you. You can clean up your Facebook account all you want, but if you really want to solidify your brand online, creating a personal website is the best way to make that happen.

This step might take you off-guard a little. Many folks think creating their own website is difficult, or that they need to learn programming, or they'd need to pay thousands of dollars to get someone else to design a website for them. The truth is that it's never been easier or cheaper to create your own website (if you're smart enough to have bought this book online than you are already computer literate enough to create your own website). If you don't know and want more details about how to easily create your own website, go to www.WebsiteFromNothing.com. It has a quick series of tutorial videos that show you how to do it.

Build your website on a domain based on your name if possible for the biggest personal branding benefit. Most names are already taken. So if your name is John Smith, you might want to register authorJohnSmith and buy www.authorjohnsmith.com, .net, and .org. Make sure your site is simple and clearly highlights your personal brand. It should clearly show your core focus. It should communicate, "This is who I am, this is what I can do, and this is why you should believe it." Be creative and take your time to update and improve your pages. It's your online real estate.

Step 6: Live your personal core brand

The last and most important step is to live your personal brand. A personal brand should be more than how you present yourself to the world. It should also be a real life description of why you're who you say you are. So that's what you should be. Spend your time emphasizing the elements of your personal brand in your life. Sometimes we don't act like the person we want the world to see. We think we're motivated, but we spend too much time watching television and surfing the internet. If you post yourself as an author and reviewer, then write every day, post interesting reviews and people will see that you are an active author and reviewer. A well thought out personal brand will help you present yourself to the world. It can also be a clear cut description for who you should aspire to be in your day-to-day life. So here's our recommendation. No matter whom you are or what your goals are, go through these steps and develop your personal brand and concentrate on the core ideals. Decide how it's going to be a part of your life. How are you going to use it to your advantage? Are you going to sit and hope that readers come to you by accident or are you are going to go and grab them?

Chapter 4

Production Tips for Selling eBooks

There are three key stages to publishing your book – production, pricing and promotion. The production of your book is as important as the storyline. If your book is already completed, then think about the content as you read this section. If you are currently writing it then try to apply some of the following production tips which will give you hooks into potential sales pockets.

1.   When *Soft Target* was written, it was a commercial entity. Yes, it was a thriller novel and the intent was to link in as many marketable hooks as possible to use at a later date. The goal was to manufacture a series so that the first book would sell further books, and vice-versa.

When marketing your books, start local, move to regional, national and eventually international. Concentrate your initial marketing on your own locality to minimize travel expenses later. If you can build a fan base in a big city or even a small town to start, then you are on a winner. Remember that word-of-mouth will sell more books than any other media. If a fan of your novels tells their family and friends that a local landmark or street name, river, cathedral or train station is in the story then they can visualize the book as it progresses. It also gives you a hook into the local media which is really important.

Try to build personal relationships with journalists, editors, radio personalities and their associates, which are priceless when you have a new book or a book signing coming up. If you don't have a publisher behind you to pay for your books to be front-on-shop in bookstores, or to make phone calls to reviewers and open doors, then you have to make contact and knock on them myself.

An important point to remember is unless you're a celebrity your book is not big news. Don't be disappointed if your local television station does not call you back or your local newspaper leaves you on hold until you finally hang up. Any successful author has had more doors slammed in their face than they can remember but as your sales grow, then so does the news value. When authors launch their first book, nobody wants to know and that is why you have to start on the bottom rung and take one step up the literary ladder at a time, working hard at building interest in you as a brand. Writing hooks into your books helps to achieve this.

2. If you have any links to large organizations, then use them in the book. At the end of *Soft Target*, the local football derby is targeted by terrorists. Liverpool is a city full of football fans, blue and red. We are talking about millions of fans. Using the clubs in the book gave it a hook into the corporate side of the clubs and they invited us to do book signings at their pre-match corporate dinners. Incorporating a scuba diving centre in the Lake District, which has thousands of members, also helped to generate sales. They distributed bookmarks and sent e-mails to their members. These tips are case specific but the key point to it is to think about the content of your book and look for the hooks which can get your foot in the door. Use the places in your book to help you reach pockets of interest.

3.   Place the names of friends, family and your main readers in them. You should use Christian names or second names only if they have asked you to put them into the storyline. If you want someone to tell everyone that they meet about your book, put them in it. Be careful not to associate their character with their names but if done correctly, this generates word of mouth and builds sales. For instance, if your brother is named Stanley Timothy Parker and you write thrillers, you might want to add in a Major in the terrorist taskforce named Stanley Timms. Another example is Sylvia Blythe, a detective in *The Child Taker*. The name is the maiden name of a big fan who also puts reviews on every novel. If you can build that kind of loyalty from readers then you will sell books to the people they talk to and good reviews are priceless. You will be amazed how many of your friends and family promise to put a review on Amazon and never get around to it.

4.   You can write a masterpiece that is worthy of literary accolades and awards the world over but if it does not speak to your target audience then you are wasting your time creating it in the first place. Be careful to keep your story flowing and the language understandable. Have you seen the Kindle apps which explain the meaning of a word to you? If you have to look up more than one word in a chapter then the writer has already lost my interest. A classic example of this is the Bourne series. The films are non-stop action and ultra-exciting but the books are difficult to read and the vocabulary is complicated. Keep it simple; the storyline is more important to the reader than your knowledge of vocabulary.

5.   Hit the ground running. You need to grab the attention of your reader in the first paragraph so they'll want to read more. If you look at your story objectively and don't believe that the first chapter excites or intrigues the reader, change it or create a prologue which does. There will be dozens of readers at book

signings who like your books because they start on page one rather than page fifty-one. Hook them on the first page and make sure that they stay hooked throughout the book.

6. Don't get too wordy. With eBooks you can provide a good amount of information in a succinct way. Resist the urge to tell too many stories unless they are specifically pertinent to the product or service that you are selling and then, only if they are applicable to the target audience. Descriptions of characters and places are important but keep the storyline flowing. Pace and plot are vital.

7. Use an eBook template to help you format the book as you write. EBook readers and apps are progressing and the quality is improving every year. Make sure when the reader opens your novel that it looks like it has come from a top flight publishing house. Most readers will check out the 'look inside this book' option which Amazon offers.

Make sure your book looks like it's been put together by a publishing professional. Include a proper title page. Check your formatting hasn't gone awry during the conversion process, leaving gaps and different font sizes where they shouldn't be. This is a common occurrence when uploading large documents. White spaces such as paragraph spaces or any use of the 'space' bar in the document can transform into "hard returns" and sentences stopping halfway across a line and continuing on the next line down and lead to gaps in the novel which look unprofessional and can put off the reader.

8. The title is important to book buyers and new readers. Make sure the title of the book is descriptive of both the genre and content of the book. It's no good writing a crime thriller called *Love and Transformation*. The title might mean a lot to you as

the author but it may mean nothing to a reader browsing the charts. One reason for the commercial success of *The Child Taker* is because the name attracts the massive female readers' market.

9. People often do judge a book by the cover. The cover is the first thing your book will be judged on. If your cover isn't eye-catching, particularly as a thumbnail, the reader or casual browser in a bookshop may by-pass it without a second glance. The cover may look brilliant when it is full size but in the eBook world it will lose its detail if it is too busy. You will see many thumbnail covers that have been knocked up on Photoshop and they do stand, but not for the right reasons. If your eBook isn't selling, why not try a new title or new cover?

The novel was originally called *Slow Burn* and while it reached top ten in the Kindle charts it didn't sell as well as *The Child Taker* - yet readers thought it was a better story. Readers' reviews explained the reason why. The cover depicts an Israeli flag burning, which readers associated with a terrorist-type novel. It is actually a tale of abuse, rape and revenge and is centered round a Jewish family, hence the flag.

One of the beauty of self-published eBooks is that you can often change and fix things in a few hours.

10. Make sure you have a catchy synopsis and back cover blurb. Do not give the plotline away but hook the readers into reading your novel. If you've any reviews or celebrity endorsements then slot short, pithy quotes from them onto the back cover.

You can also edit your product description to incorporate any new five-star reviews that you receive and keep it updated. The first thing a reader will do is read the book's summary and reviews, especially the poor ones. Make the blurb concise and exciting. Many blurbs that start with "This is a story about...." and within a few sentences, they have lost you. Read some blurbs from best-selling novels in your genre and copy their style. There is nothing wrong with following other publishers' format.

11. Create a preview. There are several ways to create a quick preview. If we mention websites that you are unfamiliar with, then go and have a quick look at them as we progress. Most of them will take less than fifteen minutes to have a virtual walk around so that you get the ideas that we're mentioning.

- Post screenshots (as images) of relevant pages alongside initial Index and content pages.

- Post relevant pages of your book alongside initial Index and content pages as html. This would also be a search engine optimized (SEO) way of promoting your eBook.

- You can use a Scribd (*www.scribd.com*) to publish and post a preview.

- You can create a Digital Flip Publication on CreateMagazines itself to publish and post a preview.

- Smashwords (*www.smashwords.com*) has a good guide on formatting which is free to download.

12. Use your eBook as the start of building a relationship with your readers. This is not the last time you will help or entertain them, but the first time. You only get one chance to make a first

impression so if you intend to write several books then it is important to get the first one right. One of the great things about the eBook market is readers can get a quick and immediate fix and when they've read something of yours they've enjoyed, they can easily buy something else at just the click of a button.

A collection of short stories at a low price is a great way to introduce readers to your style. Moreover, it doesn't cost much to have a short collection edited and doesn't take the best part of a year to write. Short stories will increase your virtual shelf-space and make you more noticeable to the reader. When *Nine Angels* was published, it was a short story written in a month, but it flew up the horror charts because of the readership that had already been established.

Choosing a Publishing Platform

13. It is very important to select the right eBook. Amazon's KDP (Kindle digital platform) is the big boy on the block and it has several key factors that you should consider before you upload your eBook to multiple sites. If you choose KDP and enroll in the Kindle prime programme, then you can offer your book free to readers for 5 days in every 90 day period. Offering your book for free opens it up to thousands and thousands of new readers. If you have multiple novels or writing a series, then it is essential.

When *The Child Taker* was offered for free for five days, over 12,000 people downloaded it. It climbed to number 2 in the Kindle free charts and when the price went back to normal, it re-entered the normal charts at number 13 and earned $1200 over the next two days.

If you choose Kindle then you have to make your book exclusive to them. There are good alternatives. A publishing platform like Zinepal (*www.zinepal.com*) creates your PDF eBook in a format that most common eBook readers can display, allowing you the virtue of uploading your eBook to multiple sites.

14. Sell your eBook through multiple eBook stores. Although top eBook stores like Amazon, Barnes & Noble and Apple account for bulk of the eBook sales, there are several smaller but equally important eBook stores which could boost your eBook sales substantially including KOBO (*www.kobobooks.com*), Books On Board (*www.booksonboard.com*), Diesel book store, and so on.

Another way to maximize sales for your eBook is to take advantage of eBook directories that accept direct submissions from authors. While most major eBook sellers like Amazon or Barnes & Noble only accept submissions from major book publishers, many of the smaller online eBook retailers or "e-tailers" will accept eBook submissions from writers. Smashwords can get your book into the big chains, if you follow their formatting policies.

15. Create a search engine optimized sales page to promote your eBook. When you are selling an eBook you are offering it via the internet. So it makes sense to have a dedicated page for your eBook which tells everything that your potential readers would want to know and thus lead to a sale. You can use this webpage to provide author information, book information, come up with special offers and have your own e-commerce system in place to sell your eBook right from your own webpage. This way you would not be sharing profits with anyone else.

When you offer your eBook for sale from eBook stores you generally end up receiving between 30-70% of your gross sales figures. The remaining amount is kept by the eBook stores as their cut. Though offering eBook through eBook stores is an absolute necessity as these stores are able to provide substantial exposure to your eBook, why not have your own sales page in place too? You can either create a simple webpage on your own, or hire a company to create one for you.

16. Make your eBook available in multiple file formats. Different users have different reading preferences. Some like to read their eBooks on a personal computer, some on an e-Book reader device like Kindle or Nook, some like to read them on new Tablet devices like iPad and some like to read them on their mobile devices. The problem is each one of these devices has its own set of compatible file formats. So it makes good sense to have your eBook in multiple file formats so that you have an extended reach and are able to provide a format compatible with several of these popular devices. Calibre is a free download program that converts your word document into eBook format accepted by most e-readers.

17. You may want to use E-Junkie for eBook delivery and for your affiliate program. It ties into PayPal (and other payment providers) and currently costs about $5 a month.

Chapter 5

Pricing Tips

This chapter is primarily for eBook authors who may have self-published their books directly on Kindle who may have more flexibility in terms of affecting the retail pricing of their eBooks, whereas eBooks published through traditional publishers tend to have the retail price set for them by the publisher. Having said that, if you feel having read this chapter that your eBook might benefit by adjusting the price, this is a discussion that you might want to have with your publisher because if you can convince them that it's going to generate more revenue for them and for you through various pricing promotions or incentives, they may try it to see if it works. Moreover, publishers always like to hear when authors are taking the initiative to help sell more copies of their books, rather than relying on the publisher to do all the sales and marketing for them.

Pricing an eBook is a real dilemma, especially with the flood of material currently on the market for free or just under a dollar. When you think of how many hours were spent on its creation, then even working on minimum wage, it should be worth thousands! After the editing, formatting and cover art has been checked, we need to look carefully at what is the best price that will likely generate the most sales? This is a question which will baffle every publisher or aspiring eBook author before they take the brave step into the digital revolution.

18. Price your eBook intelligently. This has always been a contentious issue. Many indie authors have seen success because we've been able to undercut the big boys. However, the

$.99 cent price tag has been losing some of its allure unless readers know they are buying quality. Short stories involving the characters from your novel can be offered for a low price or free in order to drum up interest in your novels.

19. It is also important not to under-price your work. A good price for novels is $2.99, novellas and short story for $1.99 or $.99 cents. As the market grows and readers switch from tree-books to eBooks the expectation of quality grows too. Readers regularly comment that the $.99 bracket belongs to self-published authors. We don't necessarily agree with that, but it is important to listen to general opinion and react accordingly.

20. If you have multiple titles, then use a low price point for your first book to hook people in to buying your others at a higher price.

21. Experiment with your prices and never be afraid to run promotions and drop the price to entice new readers. You can change the price with the click of a button.

If you are planning a launch and it is your first book, be careful not to undervalue it in the early weeks. Pick a realistic price point and stick to it for the allotted duration of the launch. If it is a new addition to your series of books, set the price slightly higher than the already published catalogue as there will be readers waiting to buy it and they will not mind paying a fair price for your new works.

Ultimately the price of the eBook is a crucial decision which only you can make. The hard fast rules of the traditional book stores do not apply here and some unorthodox approaches are allowed to experiment until you find the happy medium to be successful.

The digital world is an instant one and setting the right cost is a fluid entity. If you realise that your book and the weight that it carries will change over time and fluctuate with performance, then it will take the pressure off this issue to "get it right". If you are not happy with it, then you can change it. A new book may at first seem outlandishly priced at $9.99 but after six months of constantly being in the top tier, can easily become a bargain!

Public perception will change as your sales increase whether it is $.99 cents or $2.99. However, many successful authors are convinced that the $0.99 pricing bracket is the most successful. Remember that the most downloaded books on sale are dwarfed by the number of free eBooks available.

Trying to play safe and stick to the status-quo on pricing is a good bet but being optimistic and placing more value in your work is not a bad thing either. Try it, evaluate it and react to the results you see over a reasonable period of time. The mainstream eBook community may not legitimize an overly-optimistic approach but every marketing campaign involves some measure of trial and error, especially when it comes to pricing for digital downloads. At the end of the day, if the higher price point doesn't work, you can readily change it but only do so after a period of marketing and analysis of the results.

There is a perception out there that the huge number of eBooks being produced will dilute the amount of readers you can reach. This is nonsense. Try not to feed into the illusion of being swamped by the competition. There are far more quality eBooks being read than produced. Furthermore, the projection from Amazon, Apple, Smashwords and Forbes is eBook consumers are set to spend between $3 to $5 BILLION on eBooks in 2013, rising to a staggering $10 BILLION in 2016.

22. There is no firm and fast golden rule to eBook pricing but the key factor to consider is that an author must charge what they believe, objectively, that they themselves would pay for it. Being critical here is key, and attempting to step out of oneself and become the potential buyer should help you pick the ideal price point. You have to be realistic. If you are then why should anyone believe an eBook is worth more or less than what the author thinks?

Remember that the content rules supreme. How many stories did ancient Egyptian scribes write down? No one knows for sure, but very few written on papyrus scrolls have survived the centuries since their creation, and how much would historians pay to have those few stories? They would be priceless because of the value they place in them.

23. The length of the eBook is not as important as the content within it. The quality is what adds value, and providing a great product of some sort for the reader will dictate the value. One should never think in terms of how many words there are when pricing an eBook.

Digital downloads are much different than printed books in that generally there is a direct correspondence between page count and print costs which determine the recommended retail prices for print copies. Yet with eBooks, there are no production costs to factor in to pricing structure, and thus the "value" is based solely on quality, not quantity. This is the main reason that eBook pricing is so fluid rather than fixed, as is the case with printed versions, and why it involves careful deliberation and monitoring.

The pricing of your eBook is an important decision, and one which you can change, but once you have decided on a price it should be stuck with for a decent period of time. Changing the price every other day looks bad and may annoy readers. Use promotions, be confident and realistic and stick with your gut instinct. Your readers will soon let you know if you have got it wrong.

Chapter 6

Promotional Tips

eBook Marketing in the Virtual World

Online Marketing

When you are preparing your marketing plans, timing is crucial. If you are looking for a magic formula to sell 10,000 copies of your book, then you'll be disappointed. There is no one solution. You have to use the shotgun method, during which you are aiming multiple activities at the same target. Whether you are about to launch or re-launch your book, you have to spend some time planning all your promotional activities and making sure that you co-ordinate them for maximum effect.

24. Build up interest in your launch weeks before the actual date but make sure that your book is uploaded and available prior to the launch. Don't waste media opportunity by announcing in July that your book will be available from next Christmas

because unless you are already a household name, no one will remember.

You need to set up a checklist where you can record your activities, set completed-by dates and tick each activity off when it's accomplished. Never throw the checklist away as you can use it for reference in years to come. Keep as much detail as you can until you have experimented with the format that works for you.

As a writer, it's all too easy to become totally encapsulated in writing your next book and thus neglect your marketing plan, which is paramount to the commercial success of your book. And until you are disciplined enough to follow a monthly routine automatically use a 'to-do' list daily.

25. Do not spend any money on advertising in the press or with companies who pertain to send out press releases for you. When *Soft Target* was published as a paperback with one of the biggest international self-publishing companies around, they offered various marketing packages, which on paper looked amazing but in reality you can easily spend $5000 without seeing any tangible return on your investment.

You'll be keen and enthusiastic about getting your message to as many people as possible and paying someone to do it for you appears to be the easy option but you will more often than not waste your time and money, especially if you are an independent author. Most blanket press releases don't make it past the spam filters and as we said before, your book is not news yet.

Many authors pay a small fortune to their self-publishers and they promise to distribute press releases to newspapers and radio stations all across North American, in fact, around the world if you pay them an extra $200 only! Two years later, you'll find that you're still waiting for the phone to ring from the media sources confirming receipt of the press release and requesting an interview. Don't waste your time or money; you should do this yourself. That way, you know it's been done and it's likely to be much more effective.

Similarly, I know a self-published thriller writer who had a personal friend working in the advertising department at a glossy men's monthly magazine. It is a well-established publication with a huge readership. His friend secured him a double-page spread advertising his book for free. It sounded like an author's dream come true; two glossy pages to advertise your book with an editorial about the author and the plot. He ordered hundreds of hard copies of his novel in anticipation of the sales rush for his books. All his internet sellers were stocked up and ready to go and his eBook was uploaded and polished to perfection.

When the magazine came out, he logged online every hour on the hour to check sales. Nothing happened, in actual fact he sold less copies that month than in the month before. The advertising space would have cost him $1000s. He was absolutely devastated by the result but if he actually bought that advert, I think he would have thrown himself under the number 23 bus!

Social Media and Social Networking

26. Use the power of social media to spread the word about your eBook. The internet is the key to let an unknown author place their novel next to the biggest names in the literary world. If you use it correctly, you can generate a lot of interest in your books. If you get it wrong, you will become an annoying internet troll harassing everyone. It is a fine line, so do be careful. Be polite at all times even when people criticize your work. Remain positive and friendly or you will lose readers when you are trying to gain them and endear people to you as the author.

Social media marketing also termed as SMO has become a popular tool to promote just about everything that you can possibly think of. Sites like Twitter, Facebook, YouTube, LinkedIn, Ning, Bebo and blogs and vBlogs all allow authors to "repost" or share information about themselves and their eBook easily. Since the same information is shared by a reader with their contacts and hopefully by contacts of their contact, it helps in spreading the word fast thus reaching more and more potential readers.

Remember that bad news travels faster than good so be careful when interacting with readers. We've all read long-winded exchanges on book review sites which can make you cringe. Eventually the argument becomes the focus rather than the book or the review. Social networking sites act as word-of-mouse (viral) promotion adding more value to your book, so do not underestimate the damage you could do by being obtuse. Third-party endorsements are the best recommendation that you can hope for and readers love it when you comment on their review of your book, even if it is a poor review. Remember that they have spent their money buying your book, invested their time reading it and then taken the time to sit down and write a review. They are entitled to their opinion.

A social network facilitates regular communication between individuals who are connected by friendship or common interest. Most common interest manifests itself as a group. All you have to do is search keywords linked to your book and you will find groups to join. You can use these networks to enhance your personal network, and grow sales. The key is to use all appropriate functions of a given social network to maximum benefit.

Facebook (*www.facebook.com*) allows you to create a profile, join groups of people with similar interests, discuss your personal interests, and communicate with friends and potential customers. Facebook is massive and is a gift to the unknown author. Every author should be on Facebook.

If you already have a Facebook page then hopefully you have established the basics. Go to the "search friend" space at the top of your profile and type in 'Kindle'. Over 20 groups will appear and you need to join them all. Some of them will be invitation only but you can request an invite.

27. Build your profession into your Facebook name. For example for the co-author of this book, his is "Conrad Jones, bestselling Kindle author". That is not for vanity; it's because he wants people to know that they have found the right Conrad Jones and when he requests to join a writing group, it is obvious that he has something to offer the group.

28. When you have joined a group, make sure that you interact in a positive manner and add the other members as friends. This way your profile as a writer is growing and you are reaching dozens and dozens of people who are interested in books. Do not just join and post a link to your Amazon page and then disappear or you will turn people off you very quickly. Joining a

group for shameless self-promotion will not gain you any fans; in fact, it's likely to have the opposite effect.

29. Using the search bar, type in authors and writers, dozens of groups will appear. Join them and follow the steps above. Add their members to your friends list and remember that the more friends you have and the more interesting your posts are, the more people will be interested in you and your books. Just introduce yourself to the group and express the desire to talk to other authors and readers about writing and promoting books. Mention that you are looking for reviewers to give you feedback. Don't forget to send speedy replies to any communication you receive.

30. Once again, search. Type in 'readers' this time, but you must be careful with readers' sites. Readers' sites detest self-promotion, especially from unknown self-published authors. They can be easily offended. Join as many groups as possible and add as many friends from those groups as you can and then dedicate time every day to update and inform people about your books and launch dates by updating your profile status.

31. Increase your friends and contact list and then set up an event, which will be the launch of your eBook. Make sure you set up a Twitter (*www.twitter.com*) account and a LinkedIn (*www.linkedin.com*) site before you set up your event as they all link through the same page on Facebook. Once again, if you aren't familiar with these sites, then take ten minutes to take a look at them and familiarise yourself with how they work. It will probably take you fifteen minutes to half an hour to set yourself up with a profile when you are ready to.

32. Set up your author page on Amazon by going to the Author Central page, and link it to your Twitter and Facebook pages. All

you do is click on the icons and the software does the rest for you. Along with your blog, these three sites are crucial to any internet campaign. Build your profiles with pictures, book covers and reviews. Keep it fun and interesting and people will be regular visitors to your site.

If you are getting ready to publish a book then you have to "get up to speed" with social media marketing. A lot of authors want to learn about social media and how it's going to help them sell thousands of books but they hesitate, because they're not confident with it. They know they need to be building their author platform and brand, but don't know how Twitter fits in. It's a simple platform to send regular updates and build an audience. There are only a few things you can actually do on Twitter but simple is good. Everything else that flows from your involvement with it comes from the network of people you connect with.

It takes time and effort to build a following. If you have no followers then you are wasting your time. You have to grow a community around the value of the content and ideas you share on the site.

33. On Twitter, make sure your username name is not random or too long; 10 or 12 characters should do. Remember that your username on Twitter needs to include author or writer in it if you're going to use it for promoting your book. It is part of your branding strategy.

34. There is free software that makes Twitter a lot easier to use. Twitterific on the iPad and the iPhone are good, though there are many others so it's worth looking around to see what works for you. The software allows you to automate your Twitter profile which saves time.

Being able to schedule Tweets in advance is a big advantage and you can auto-tweet, which gives you the ability to plan a campaign.

Here are some pointers for using Twitter.

1) Don't read EVERY tweet.

2) Follow anyone who follows you (and unfollow spammers).

3) Promote other people 12x to every 1 self-promotional tweet.

4) Build lists to watch people who matter to you more closely.

5) Retweet the good stuff from others. Sharing is caring.

6) A lot of @replies shows a lot of humanity and engagement.

7) Robot tweets are less effective than human tweets.

8) Promote the new/less followed authors more than the well-established "names."

9) Set an egg timer. Twitter is addictive.

10) Everyone tweets their own way. You're doing it wrong, too - to someone.

The same principles that apply to social media apply to social networking in general, especially in terms of building up a group of readers who are keen to hear about your publishing plans.

35. Search out people in the book world as you did online. Target your searches to find the people with the biggest followings in your genre. Once you find them, you can start looking through the list of who they are following to find more people to follow. Build up your followers, which takes time, by planning a launch well in advance. Even if you have already launched, set up your profile and spend time regularly building followers.

36. Search the list pages too. There are many eBook review groups and eBook retweeting groups. Some will have over 100,000 followers so if they pick up one of your promotional tweets and pass it on, the results are incredible. There are many writers and publishers who you can follow for great information and tips. Try to find lists created by experts in your field and retweet any useful links to your followers.

37. If we assume that you are now following important people in your niche, you should check them out on a daily basis. Remember to keep adding followers too. Keep your focus tight at first so you don't overwhelm yourself with input. Read the tweets from these industry leaders and add the people with lots of followers. Click through anything that looks interesting to see what they are linking to. Watch especially for links that get retweeted or passed along.

38. There's no rush. You might want to read tweets for two or three months before sending out any tweets of your own. Be patient and keep watching and soon you'll see why some people are popular and lots of people want to follow them. It is usually because they consistently provide links and ideas that are valuable; or because they make an effort to connect with people individually.

39. Once you've worked out what's considered valuable in the communities you're following, it's time to become a participant. Do a little searching and see if you can find resources that have not been mentioned recently and pass it on. If you use your Facebook account to post links then it'll automatically send it to Twitter and LinkedIn. Create a short tweet alerting people to this resource, put in a shortened link and tweet it. You will pick up followers if your content is useful.

40. Retweet other authors as this builds brand loyalty. This is all about sharing discoveries, sharing content and not about direct selling. You are building trust and a trusted community of followers; at the same time you are receiving valuable tips from the people you are following.

41. Be polite to all even when abuse is tweeted in your direction. There are thousands of trolls out there with nothing better to do than annoy people on the internet. If you encounter them, be professional. You will gain the respect of the rest of the community if you handle yourself with dignity. Remember that others can see your conversations unless they are private messages and abusive arguments in clear view of the community will alienate your readers.

In essence, you are asking people that you never met to trust you and read your eBook. This is done most effectively by adding value to others and not by tweeting anything you have not personally verified yourself. Trust is the most important element in the community you are building.

42. Twitter is truly an amazing phenomenon, considering it only consists of 140 characters of basic text. Become familiar with posting links and photographs. They will create interest in you and your book. The creativity, the energy and vitality on Twitter is astonishing. It can be a great place to connect to people who are interested in your work, and who in turn will send your message out into their own networks of followers.

43. Join LinkedIn and follow the same principles as the Facebook tips but remember that LinkedIn is a professional site for executives and senior management from every industry. There are a multitude of author groups, publishers groups, self-publishers, agents and marketing forums. The site gives you the facility to invite everyone in your email address list to join your network by simply clicking one button. The author groups and marketing forums are extremely vibrant and useful.

44. Join marketing groups and as many book-related forums as you can. Set aside half an hour everyday to participate in the forums. Read the discussions in the marketing forums as there are hundreds of people asking the same questions as you are. There is a plethora of information to be learned on this site and people are very quick to point out any pitfalls that they have fallen into. Learning from other authors' mistakes is a valuable exercise.

45. Link your LinkedIn account to your Twitter and Facebook accounts. They will synchronize at the click of an icon, which saves you a lot of time and effort. These channels thrive on authentic social interactions, so be careful not to overtly sell

yourself or your eBook to avoid alienating the connections you make. For example, rather than posting multiple messages about your eBook being available for sale, try to contribute meaningful dialogue in conversations about relevant and related topics. This will position you as an intelligent writer, which will help build your author brand.

Be careful not to hassle agents and publishers. I have seen some cringe-worthy conversations between disparaging, know-it-all writers and not-so desperate agents. They tend to be short, one-sided affairs with abrupt endings!

Talk about your eBook in an open forum intelligently and realistically. Don't claim to have sold 10k copies of your eBook when your Amazon ranking proves that you have sold ten. You can share any genuine reviews that you receive and post links to your eBook, which gives your target audience the chance to glance at your work and make up their own minds as to its merits.

LinkedIn is a useful tool for making business connections and meeting other authors, but remember that it is just another tool in the box. Even the most active users miss on some simple ways to optimize the way they use LinkedIn.

Below are a few more tips on how to make the most of your LinkedIn presence.

a) Think about your goals. Why are you on LinkedIn? Is it to find new readers and other authors? To be found? Some mix of the two? Your goals should drive your entire presence on the site.

b) Post a picture of your face. You should have a professional-looking headshot as your LinkedIn photo so people can put a name to a face. If you're uncomfortable with readers or prospective agents seeing your picture next to your professional credentials (a valid concern), you can change your privacy settings so only your connections can see your photo.

c) Use LinkedIn to help remember names. LinkedIn can help you with offline networking too. Simply checking on someone's profile after meeting them at a networking event, even if you don't connect, can help you remember their name and what they do. This is another reason why having a picture is important—it will help people remember you.

d) Make the most of your LinkedIn headline. Your headline does not have to be your job title alone. Keep it concise, but make sure that it conveys what you do and what your skills are.

e) Post status. Updating your status gives you visibility on your connections' LinkedIn home page. If you have found something online you think your business connections would like, or you have good news to share about your work, spread the word by posting it on LinkedIn.

f)   Write a content-rich but concise summary. Your summary should be about you, not your book. Use concrete details like results you have generated and the work you do on a daily basis to show people how professional you are, not tell them.

g) Explore various LinkedIn applications. Add Amazon's Reading List application to your LinkedIn profiles. If you are not sure how the fiction you read is relevant to your professional connections, think again. You may receive more comments on this list than anything else in your profile.

h)   Add sections to your profile. LinkedIn offers several sections beyond the standards so users can showcase their volunteer experience, projects, foreign languages, even test scores. This is especially helpful for new networkers who may not have extensive work experience outside of writing a book. Adding more sections an add weight to any profile.

i) Connect with care. Your network is only as valuable as the strength of your connections. For some professionals, it is advantageous to connect generally, but I tend to favor smaller useful lists. If you would like to connect with someone and think it might be a stretch, be sure to personalize the message you send with the invite to explain why you want to connect and why this person should want to connect with you.

j) Join and participate in discussion groups. Some groups are full of spam, drivel and dross, but others are generally valuable. For example, in the book marketing groups there are great places to get and give free advice. Do a little research, think back to your goals, and you'll likely find groups that will help you reach them. If you can't find a group, just start one!

46. There are many similar general-interest networks like MySpace, Ning, and Bebo, and video sharing websites like YouTube which are essential as you progress, each with different functions and advantages. YouTube is ideal for posting book trailers, linking to any footage of television appearances or advertising clips you produce yourself promoting your eBook.

47. If you're planning a series of books with a serial protagonist, try creating a Facebook or Twitter account for your protagonist and hold conversations in the voice of that character. The Jack Reacher (Lee Child) forums are constantly busy with readers and avid fans discussing the fictional hero as if he's real. It is not everyone's cup of tea but it works for several authors.

48. There are networks designed to connect business professionals such as Plaxo, Ryze and most recently BranchOut (a Facebook/LinkedIn hybrid). You can target some networks based on the content of your book. Follow the steps for your Facebook profile. The sites are linked so you might as well take full advantage of the exposure they can offer.

49. Link with as many other authors as you can. To communicate with other authors and avid readers, try Shelfari or weRead where you can rate, review, and discuss your book, as well as books by other authors. Use Meetup to find and join groups united by a common interest such as politics, books, games, movies, careers, or hobbies. Sites like Digg, Pinterest, Delicious, StumbleUpon, Buzzfeed, Slashdot and Reddit are social bookmarking services for storing, sharing and discovering popular content. Find and use the best ones for your book

50. Affiliate programs offered by sites like ClickBank and Tradebit can also help you to market your eBook as they provide online marketplaces for digital information products. The sites aim to serve as a connection between digital content creators (known as "vendors") and affiliate marketers, who then promote the relevant content to consumers.

51. Don't spend much on Google adwords and other "pay-per-click" traffic generators. I have seen campaigns run by authors who have a lot more marketing money than most fall flat on their face. Remember that free advertising is the best way to raise your literary profile and build up a readership for your eBook.

Blogging and vBlogging

52. You need a good blog because people want "conversation" about the topic of your eBook. It will also help you in Google ratings. A blog builds relationships and credibility. It helps to use Facebook for short daily updates as they are shared automatically with other sites and then if people are interested

in your posts, they will interact. This is a great way for building up links with both readers and writers. You can use your blog to build your platform, exposure, and credibility as an expert on your topic. Keep it authentic, post to it regularly and respond to visitor comments quickly and professionally.

If you cannot commit to writing a regular blog, consider creating occasional content for other blogs which pertain to the topic of your book. Reach out to similar bloggers for guest blog opportunities, and invite them to be a guest on your blog. To get started blogging, consider using a template provided by services like Wordpress, and feature your blog on your website.

Some authors find video blogs (or vBlogs) useful in selling their eBooks. There are three main components. The first is vBlog software. There are a number of options in this regard. Blogger is commonly used by many as it is a free and hosted service, but to make Blogger work you'll have to know or learn some basic computer programming (HTML). Alternatively, if you're willing to pay a nominal fee, you can try TypePad which has more features and is easier to use.

The second component is another hosted service called vBlog Central which hosts photos and videos, automatically converts the videos into Windows, QuickTime, and Real formats, and can automatically link them to your blog.

The third part is actually creating the video itself, preferably with a digital video camcorder with professional editing functionality so that you can ensure your video is the best it can be.

53. Remember, whatever promotional material you decide to release in support of your eBook will be a reflection on your eBook. If you produce an unedited, unprofessional Youtube video or vBlog to showcase your book, it can put readers off. If you own a shop and have an amateurish-looking shop window display, it's not going to draw people in. Your book promotion should be as professional as your book display.

Reviews and Endorsements

54. Get your eBooks reviewed by as many friends and family members as you can. Books with published reviews and real testimonials from various eBook stores or your readers tend to get more attention and interest and thus sell more. Try and reply to every review, good or bad. If it is good then you can build a rapport with the reviewer, which tends to generate more positive reviews from them in the future.

If they are scathing then either ignore it, or be polite and thank them for the time they spent reading your book. We have all seen hilarious discussion threads between wounded authors and reviewers. Some of them are very heated and almost abusive, but at the end of the day their opinion is just that, their opinion. You cannot change that.

One best-selling thriller writer was banned from Amazon recently because of his constant battles and criticism of negative reviewers. Moreover, he was uploading negative reviews of his competitors' books on Amazon, thereby lowering them in the Amazon search engine results, which is a practice known as "sock puppeting." Don't ever do this. The long-term result was that the author turned hundreds, if not thousands of potential readers, off his books. As mentioned earlier, your brand is both you and the book. If readers don't like you, then they won't buy, endorse or recommend your books; it's simple as that.

Tips for getting reviews on Amazon and Goodreads

When readers shop for books on Amazon.com and other online bookstores, many of them read the book reviews before they make a purchase. Even if they came to the site to buy a particular book, they may read the reviews to verify that they are making a good selection and the reviews can affect their decision to purchase or not especially if the price is prohibitive. For 99c, they will take the gamble but for $4.99 they may rely on the reviews which have been posted to help make a decision.

Positive reviews are a great selling point for all types of books, but they are especially important for nonfiction books, where consumers often compare several books on the same topic. Amazon actually encourages this, by displaying other similar books on your book's sales page. The entire system is linked by customers who buy this book, also buy this one and someone who reviewed this book also purchased a book by this author etc.

So, what's the secret to getting great book reviews on Amazon (besides writing a great book)? Ask people who have read your book to post reviews and make it easy and less time consuming for them by providing a link to your book page on Amazon.com. We have lost count of the number of friends and family who promised to write a review and never have. Their time is precious and your book is not top of mind so send the link to make it easier for them. Amazon is by far the largest online bookseller. Anyone who has an Amazon user name and password and has purchased any product on Amazon.com can review your book there, even if they purchased your book elsewhere or received a free complimentary review copy so asking in a polite, professional manner is only going to help.

Here are several easy ways to invite people to post reviews for you:

If you send out review copies to colleagues and bloggers seeking reviews, ask them if they will also post the review on Goodreads or a brief review on Amazon.

If someone writes a positive review of your book on Facebook or another site, ask them to post it on Amazon. Before contacting the reviewer, check to see if they have already posted the review and then send them the link to do it.

When you receive an email or other correspondence praising your book, reply with a thoughtful request to post a book review on Amazon along with the link. If someone has taken the time to write to you about your book, they are obviously a fan and will probably be happy to post a book review for you. Here's a sample message which you could adapt to help you when you receive a comment on Facebook for instance:

"Hey there, thanks so much for the review. I am so pleased that you enjoyed my book. I wonder if you would be kind enough to spend a few minutes posting your thoughts on Amazon for me as good reviews really help book sales. To post your comments or a brief review on my Amazon page atwww.Amazon.com/mybookpage. Look for the "customer reviews" section about halfway down the page and click on the

"create your own review" button to the right. Or, use this link to go directly to the review form: http://yourshortlink.com.

If you're a Barnes & Noble customer, click the "write a review" button at www.BarnesAndNoble.com/mybookpage ."

There is nothing wrong with asking family members and friends to post a review (or they may offer to do so), but be careful that they have actually read it. There has been a lot of bad publicity aimed at well-known authors who have used fake internet identities to review their own books. If suspected, others will find out and they can do considerable damage to your credibility and reputation. Be careful because anyone who shares your last name (unless it's a really common name) will look like a relative.

Also, you don't want the reviews to sound contrived. For example, posting something like, 'My sister Betsy wrote this brilliant book, I'm so proud of her. It's the best book of all time!' is not a good idea and could look a little suspicious! And of course you want these folks to post an honest opinion – you might ask them to write a couple of sentences stating what they liked best about the plot. Positive book reviews on Amazon and other online bookstores can boost your sales – take the initiative to ask for reviews and you'll be rewarded.

Another possibility is to seek out reviewers who have reviewed books on similar or related topics or in your genre on Amazon and ask them if they are interested in reviewing your book. You may be able to get the reviewer's contact information by clicking on their name and looking for their website or blog address on their Amazon profile.

Should you write a review of your own book? Definitely not! Not even to communicate to your readers. Whatever you write, you will have to give it a star rating and in doing so you will turn many readers off or cause them to question the validity of your other reviews. It's never been a better time to be a self-published author or traditionally published author, and there have never been more book reviewers available to the writer who decides to go and look for reviews. Book reviewers help spread the message about your book by publishing a review to their own network some of which run into the hundreds of thousands.

How to reach out to the book bloggers to review your book

First you need to gather all the information that a reviewer will need in order to save them time and be more inclined to review your work. Here is what you will need.

- Complete PDF of your book. Either include the covers if you can, or have the cover available as a separate JPG file attached
- Print copies and mailing supplies. If you're publishing via print-on-demand, order enough books to respond to reviewer requests quickly or if you are traditionally published, speak to your publishers about review copies. Many publishers will send them free of charge on request.
- Press release about the launch of your book. Try to make it sound like a story you would read in the newspaper.
- Cover letter. This should be a brief introduction to you and your book, but keep it short.
- Photos of the book and author. You'll need high- and low-resolution images if you're approaching both print and online reviewers.

- Author bio. This is a good place to show your qualifications, particularly if you're a nonfiction author.

There are literally thousands of book bloggers online, and most of them review books for free. Many of them have faithful followings and are thoughtful reviewers and good writers. There are also reviewers offering paid reviews but you might want to avoid them altogether, as there are no good reasons to pay for a review.

- One of the best new references to find reviewers online is the list put together and indie author from Step-by-Step Self-Publishing.
- Midwest Book Review welcomes self-published books, and their website is a wealth of information on reviews.
- Indie Reader, a new website, invites authors to submit their books for review, and they have published over 150 reviews on their site already.
- Self-Publishing Review also allows reviewers to post book reviews, and members (just an opt-in) can post to the site.
- Some of the online writer's forums and community sites are great places to look for reviewers. Absolute Write is a favorite, but don't overlook newer communities like forums.
- Book Blogs, a site for book bloggers, has over 1,500 bloggers who say they review books. It's a good place to explore.

Once you have your material organised then follow these steps and make sure that you pick the right reviewers. Find out what kind of books the reviewer likes to review, and only select appropriate reviewers.

Query the reviewers. Check each reviewer's requirements. Some want you to just send the book, but many ask for a query. Some review e-books, many do not. Conforming to their requirements saves both of you time.

Send the book. In your query make sure to offer both versions of the book, the PDF and the print copy, or both.

Follow up. Don't stalk or harass the reviewer, who is probably doing this in her spare time. But if you haven't heard anything after a few weeks, follow up to see if they still intend to write the review.

Thank the reviewer. It's common courtesy, but it also shows you appreciate the time and effort someone else took to help bring your book to the attention of more people. Book reviews can be very effective in spreading the word about a good book. Nothing sells books as well as a good recommendation, and you can get people talking about your book if you can bring it to their notice

Bundling Content & Giveaways

55. Offer limited period discounts and create bundles. Just like any e-commerce product, an eBook can be offered at a reduced rate for a short time or combine with related products to increase the overall value or worth of the deal to the user.

56. Build a loyal customer base with a plan to write a series of novels and let people know that there will be more to come. Listen to your readers and give them what they ask for. One main virtue of publishing eBooks is you can turn them out much quicker than traditionally published books. And if you're adept

enough to develop an avid fan base, you have the benefit of knowing exactly what they want next.

On a related note, communicate directly with your readers, and communicate with them often. Write back to each of the fans who have written to you over the years — keep all of their messages — to let them know about the book and your plans for your next book. Listen to your avid readers, keep them happy and they'll return to buy your books time and time again.

57. Another marketing strategy is to give away the first chapter free on sites like Mass-EBooks, but include a bold link and a call to action in the chapter telling people how to buy the rest of the eBook. Make sure that you do this for a limited period, as free or discounted offers for eBooks that seem to go on and on can actually diminish your brand name.

Chapter 7

Promotional Tips

eBook Marketing in the Real World

Offline Marketing

This section explains how to build interest in yourself and your eBook in the real world as opposed to the virtual, using a small marketing budget.

58. Search the internet and local directories to find groups and associations that might be interested in your eBook and the story behind its creation. Sit down and write a list of places and people that you associate your past with. It doesn't matter how tenuous the links are - write them down. Include where you went to school, colleges, university, chess clubs, scout groups, Irish dancing classes! It doesn't matter how brief your association was, write down everything that comes into your head. I found that people were proud that an ex-pupil, ex-member, ex-student has become a published author and the opportunities which come from contacting them in a professional manner, are endless. Many will invite you to speak to their current pupils, members etc and even if they don't, some

of them will tell their families and friends who will buy your books out of curiosity.

59. Contact the local press in the towns that you have links with. When Conrad published his first book, he received coverage from the Holyhead and Anglesey Mail and The North Wales Chronicle which boasted how a local man was launching his first novel and that Holyhead was one of the settings in the book. There were multiple links there because he was a Holyhead author and the port was integral to the plot.

The same month, the St Helens Reporter carried a story about a local author, whose family went back generations in the town, launching his first eBook. Conrad was born there, so they claimed him as theirs! The Chester Chronicle covered the story, as did the Warrington papers and the Liverpool editions. The Manchester Evening News also published a half-page article. He used the hook that he was loyal to that area and his book was forged from the burglary which had rendered him unemployed. It wasn't just a book launch written by an unknown, it had become a human interest story.

Once they have published an article about you, they are keen for updates. Be careful not to bother journalists too often. Keep your updates limited to real news, such as reaching #10 in the charts or releasing a new novel. The point is that three cities and several large towns are now on his media list when he has a new novel coming out. Nine times out of ten, they print updates when he contacts them.

My other hook was the IRA bombing of Warrington Bridge Street in 1993. Conrad was an assistant manager at the Bridge St McDonalds when two bombs exploded just after 12 noon. The explosions were directly outside the store and two young boys died that day. Once we evacuated the restaurant, some people tried to administer first aid to the bomb victims.

Conrad was deeply affected by the events of that day and it sparked an interest which became the basis to his writing years later. He read anything he could get his hands on about terrorists and criminal gangs and their baneful motivations. *Soft Target* was inspired by the events of that day. His biography indicates where his inspiration came from and again, it is a powerful human interest angle from which a journalist can pitch a story.

When you are looking for hooks into your eBook, think about your life and how you can hook people into it.

60. You can contact schools by writing letters to their English departments and offering your time to talk to their pupils about writing and publishing books. Don't pester anybody with e-mails or phone calls. Take the time to write detailed personal letters and then leave it to them to contact. In the world of technology that we live in, there is still nothing to match the impact of a well-written personalized letter.

61. Contact schools and colleges in all the towns that you mentioned in your eBook. Pitch your presentations along the lines of why and how you wrote the book rather than the storyline. That way you can hold the interest of readers and non-readers. All of a sudden your book sales will begin to rise even before they actually appear anywhere. It will be obvious that teachers and their associates are buying your book out of interest and your fan base and readership will continue growing, with is key to your long-term success as a writer.

62. The next stage is to step outside of the personal arena. Look for anywhere that large groups gathered for meetings. Seek out associations in the areas you have links with. Conrad chose Rotary Clubs to begin with. There are six around Warrington alone and over twenty in and around Liverpool. Once he had contacted them, he moved on to Chester, St Helens and Northern areas. This association consists of men mostly over retirement age. They have plenty of time to read. Most of the chapters meet once a week and they invite speakers to their dinners. The majority of speakers are looking for donations from the Rotary Club for one cause or another so a speaker with a human interest story was like a breath of fresh air to them. Soon his Rotary connections were inviting him to speak at joint dinner events which consist of the male organization and the female members who are known as the Inner Wheel. Now the gatherings were reaching over 50 people, sometimes more, and and his book sales were growing rapidly.

63. There are thousands of creative writing groups across the country and you can target them too. Be careful if you approach these groups. Draft an interesting letter of introduction and offer your time for free. You will get your expenses paid when they buy your books and tell their friends about you.

You may have a lukewarm response from writing groups because of being self-published. There are lots of people who don't class independent authors as credible authors. They think that if you couldn't find a publisher, then it is because your book is not good enough, when in fact there are many talented authors who never get a represented by established literary agents or traditional publishers until and unless they're already well-known. It's a real catch-22 which many authors know all too well. J. K. Rowling received numerous rejections from publishers, not because her book was about a young boy named Harry wasn't good enough, but because of publishers' reluctance to invest in unknown authors. Once you build up your author platform and author brand, more publishers will seriously consider publishing your work.

64. Similarly, there are thousands of reading groups, mostly based in libraries. Contact all the libraries in all the towns that that you can and ask to speak to them. When you have positive feedback from a reading group, the library will order more copies of your books for the entire group to read. This applies to eBooks as well as tree-books. If you speak to a library group, it usually lasts all night! They love asking questions and talking about writing and books. Be careful to schedule enough time to talk to these groups at your leisure so that you don't offend anyone by constantly checking your watch or rushing off.

65. Find out how many people are expected, leave a gift behind and never ask for any money in return. Remember that selling and marketing are two different entities. You are trying to build interest and loyalty in your brand name and a small inexpensive gift connected to your book will always be well-received. Search online for bookmarks and postcards as there are several sites where you can purchase quality products at a reasonable price; if you have a few hundred pounds to spare then that's fine; buy quality bookmarks. You can get buy postcards with your book cover printed on them from online printers done inexpensively.

You don't have to increase your overheads further as travelling and eating out can be costly enough. In fact, you can use your own laptop to design bookmarks and thin sheets of card to print them on. If you are talking to your local Community Club, you can download their logo and put your book covers on one side and their logo on the reverse. You can do the same with football clubs, libraries, schools and colleges. Cut the bookmarks neatly so that they look professional. At every presentation, make sure that everyone receives one and leave some for any members who were unable to attend.

66. Make sure your contact details and your website and any other relevant book links are printed on any promotional material you use, and that the information is up-to-date. Some people wanted them signed which is great as you cannot sign an eBook!

67. Wherever you go, make sure that people know that you can be found on Facebook and Twitter and leave your email address. Print your profile details and web addresses on each bookmark. That way you will build a working contact list which you can use to promote your next book launch or book signing event. If you build a relationship with people, then they will be interested in what you are doing next.

68. Another benefit of eBooks is you can see your sales and sales rankings on an hourly basis. Set yourself a time every day when you check and monitor your figures. The overnight sales tend to update at about ten o'clock the next morning. Hopefully you will see the sales spikes following your promotional activities. For instance, if you have an after-dinner speaking engagement on a Thursday night, you'll see your books climbing up the rankings on Friday.

Track your figures. You cannot react to sales decreases if you don't know that they are decreasing! Keep a record of what works and what doesn't work as it will save you time and effort later on. Don't waste your valuable time on individuals or groups who do not buy into your message. Move on and concentrate on the next function.

Remember as an author, you have to develop a thick skin. Not everyone will like your book and you'll become accustomed to people hanging up the telephone or being patronizing and condescending. Take it on the chin; it's nothing personal and you will probably never see them again.

Measure your sales rankings against your actual book sales. You will soon be able to look at the rankings and gauge roughly how many books you have sold. It is exciting watching your book sell but don't waste too much time on it. Be careful not to get too fixated on the sales reports as it easy to spend hours every day looking to see if you have sold another book when you could be focusing on your writing or marketing. Building sales and generating public interest is a long-term venture. It will not happen overnight.

69. Marketing your book is a journey and as with most journeys, if you have no idea where you are going, you're unlikely to know when you are on the right road or when you've arrived. That's why goals are important. Set yourself a realistic goal but remember to be specific and keep your goals measurable. For example, becoming a bestseller within a year is not realistic and you will find it hard to measure on a daily or weekly basis.

- For sales, use the reports that you receive from retailers or distributors and keep a spreadsheet of results.

- For readership, you can send readers to a website or blog for additional information or interaction and use analytics provided by the site to measure traffic.

- For interest, look at whether other people start to quote you and mention your ideas, and how often your blog or Twitter posts are forwarded by others.

- For revenue goals, keep track of the profit from your eBook. You may have incurred expenses in getting your book to market, and by tracking this you'll know exactly when your book becomes profitable. Once you have cleared your production costs, you are earning a residual income while you sleep, but only if you put the effort in to market it while you're awake.

70. Think seriously about printing a small number of your book using sites like Lulu.com or Createspace. They are simple and easy to use and you can carry a number of hard copies to your promotional appearances but be selective who you give them to. Your expenses will increase and your brand may suffer if you hand them out randomly. Remember you're looking for exposure for your eBook primarily but not everyone who you meet will be an avid eBook reader.

Use your hard copies to encourage reviews from within your media list. If you manage to get a piece in your local newspaper, then send the journalist a signed hard copy. You cannot have enough reviews on your books and if it costs you the price of a print-on-demand book, then it is worth every penny. Being a successful independent author means taking a long-term view. Many marketing efforts take months or years to come to fruition.

As you market your eBook, you will start to think of other ways to adapt the basics to your own circumstances. Keep thinking of how you can apply the successful promotions that you use to other groups or associations in different towns and cities.

71. Developing an author website that is fully functional, easy to navigate and consistently updated to showcase your work is essential in a digital age. It is your online profile describing you and your book in your own words. If it is clear and professional then it is building your credibility as an author. Your website should be updated often, and it's a good idea to link your Facebook and Twitter pages so you can send one message to all your profiles at once. Your website can also be your shop window through which you can sell your books. If you'd prefer, you can link to your Amazon or Kobo pages so that you don't have to fulfill orders yourself. A well-designed website adds credence in your business and brand as an established author.

Reserve a domain name that includes your name and the title of your book. There are dozens of free hosting sites. Design your site to raise your profile and sell copies of your eBook; show your book covers and describe how your reviews are going. If you write fiction, be sure to describe your plot in compelling terms and add links to your readers' reviews. Use your website to promote your book by providing links to retail outlets. You may also choose to sell your book directly on your site and offer incentives such as free shipping, a limited-time offer or a special price for an autographed book. A website provides an unique opportunity to show your biographical details, positive reviews, endorsements and testimonials.

72. As your sales grow and your book climbs the ranking, use your press contacts to inform their readers about your progression. Reasonably modest downloads can get your book into the genre charts and that is newsworthy. If the press is impressed and pick up your updates, it fosters viral marketing.

73.   When planning your outreach, think about your target readers. What media do they watch, listen to, or read? You can reach a large number of people in a relatively short period of time through broadcast appearances on TV and radio shows, print, and online media. Publicity is typically free and targeted to journalists, editors, and producers at media outlets. Media personnel are looking for a story, so you and your eBook could potentially provide them with a new storyline, background information, and other material.

A few years ago a former colleague, Simon Gould, asked Conrad to help promote his debut novel, *Playing the Game*. He followed the eBook techniques which launched the *Soft Target* series and within a few months, his book was #4 in the Kindle charts. Not genre-specific, but the overall charts. He sold 40,000 downloads in a few months. His success was newsworthy and he began riding the media interest and his book continued to sell. National television contacted him following an enquiry he made and asked about eBooks and how he achieved his level of success. He mentioned Conrad's role and they sent a camera team and interviewed both Simon and Conrad.

The interviews were televised on the evening news at six o'clock, nine o'clock and ten o'clock. Unfortunately for Simon, the piece didn't show the title of his book. It was more about the eBook phenomenon but they concentrated much of the item on Conrad's books. It was cruel because Simon had contacted them, but the following day *Soft Target* was back in the top 20. The point is if you keep casting the net widely with interesting topics and timely updates, you will eventually catch fish... even if you have to share it with your mate!

74.   Draft your own press release and make sure your regular updates to the media are professional and interesting. The basic press release is a brief description that presents the most

newsworthy aspect of your book – the "hook" - in an interesting way, for example, reaching #10 in the thriller sales charts!

An effective press release uses an attention-grabbing headline and lead paragraph. It is also free of advertising or overt commercialism. Subsequent sections should include background information and other details that help put the newsworthiness of the story into perspective.

There should be a few paragraphs about the book, a brief about the author, and an action-filled excerpt from the book about a half page in length. Then, you should include your website address (or Amazon link) where the book can be ordered, and contact details for any press enquiries.

There are various free PR websites and online newswires where you can upload your press release, including:

www.free-press-releases.com
www.i-newswire.com
www.24-7pressrelease.com
www.clickpress.com
www.express-press-release.com
www.prlog.org
www.free-press-release-center.info.
www.nosyjoe.com
www.sanepr.com
www.your-story.org
www.pr.com

It usually takes 2 – 3 days before the press releases appear online as some PR websites may want to check them firstly before uploading them.

You should include copies of the latest press release in your press pack. Rather than issuing one press release only about the publication of your book, drip feed the media with periodic press releases that stimulate public interest and invite reviews and interviews. You can write book releases about upcoming speaking engagements, festival talks, future book signings, success in writing competitions, and any other newsworthy events related to your book.

75. After becoming comfortable with basic publicity, you can begin more concerted and targeted efforts to reach media outside of your local area. Create an informative press pack that has information about your book and why it is important to the outlet's audience. Include testimonials and a list of the topics you can discuss. When targeting the media, it's often beneficial to start locally and then broaden your scope.

Finally, look the part of a successful author by dressing smart and professionally and using body language and posture effectively.

76. If you do not feel comfortable talking to reporters or conducting radio and television interviews, then stick to print and online media. This type of exposure is equally important, particularly if you're camera shy. This includes newspapers, magazine, ezines, newsletters, and trade journals, most of which will have well-trafficked websites. Approach journalists the same way you would approach producers, with a press kit written to the needs of their readers. Contact them to review your book, suggest a story or interview on you and your book, or offer to contribute some useful content to them. Be selective, starting with the media most likely to help your eBook reach your target audience. Follow up consistently and professionally.

77. Direct marketing is a general form of communication that enables you to reach a targeted audience directly through one or more channels. Examples include email, direct mail, catalogues, and promotional letters. Postcards and bookmarks can also be effective since the message is seen immediately without opening an envelope or email.

In all cases, direct marketing materials can be sent to a targeted list of potential buyers, and responses can be measured. With both email and postal marketing campaigns, it is important to make sure your direct marketing material stands out and grabs the recipients' attention. With email, the subject line is critical. Similarly, you can write a teaser on an envelope to entice the recipient to open the envelope. In postal mail, send a cover letter, sales piece, and some means for the recipient to respond such as a business reply card (BRC). Make an offer that will get the recipient to act quickly, such as directing them to your website to see a sample chapter or offering a free gift or autographed copy with a response by a certain date.

78. When you have a target market, you can reach it through personal communication. The major benefit of personal marketing is that you get immediate feedback as to how well your message is getting through. It will also give you an opportunity to answer questions and close sales. When you're selling your books, you're also selling yourself as an author, so personal marketing is a great way to build your authentic author brand through direct and directive communication. Examples of personal marketing initiatives are bookstore signing events, launch parties, book tours, speaking events, and personal presentations at libraries.

79. Practice and polish your presentations. Practice projecting your words and using your body language to evoke the sort of response that you'd like. While you'd use professional selling

techniques when direct selling, be sure not to come off too "commercial" as that can put off potential readers.

80. If you are getting excellent reviews and positive feedback on your eBook then consider entering it into competitions. There are various award competitions for most kinds of books. Awards can focus on your book's cover design, content, marketing, sales and productivity, and even editing. There are awards for a range of genres including business, inspirational, crime fiction, fantasy, literary fiction, science-fiction, women's fiction and children's books. Winning, being shortlisted, long-listed or just nominated for an award is a newsworthy event and has many benefits, including increased exposure, greater kudos and credibility, and potential for testimonials and sales.

An element of personal satisfaction and validation comes with receiving awards as well. When you win an award, make the most of it! Mention the award in your literature, e-mail signature, business cards, postcards, website, and letterhead. Describe your award in your press kits and include it in press releases or any display materials for in-person events.

81. There are many literary festivals, book fairs and trade shows to add to your diary. They are great events for networking and getting your face seen and your voice heard. They give you the chance to network with people in the industry, meet potential new readers, generate sales leads, close sales, research trends, and build relationships, foster direct sales opportunities, generate publicity, or launch a new title.

82. Enlist your friends and family to distribute your postcards and bookmarks to their workmates. Each town has its center with and you can promote your book there with great effect, and hand out and electronically distribute promotional material

through your companies' internal e-mail systems. Don't wait for your friends and colleagues to offer to help. Rather, take the initiative and ask if they can recommend your book to others.

Chapter 8

Promotional Tips

eBook Marketing – Other Resources

83. Join Goodreads.com and build up your profile as a reviewer as well as an author. You can add all the classics that you have read and write a quick review on them. Add other authors as friends and invite them to swap reviews on your book. Make sure that you are positive. It is better not to leave a review than to leave a poor one.

84. Join Kindleboards. It is the biggest Kindle forum on the internet and there are hundreds of forums and groups to interact with. The same rules apply here as aforementioned - don't ram your book down people's throats. Develop your contacts and be constructive and gregarious.

85. Can your eBook be adapted to another market or format? Conrad turned six of his thrillers into Young Adult novels by taking out any abusive language and toning down the violence. If you can do that then it is a quick and simple exercise, as teenagers love exciting books and they tend to be active on social networks and have a large peer group to spread the word about your books.

86. Set up outposts which are profiles and different sites and monitor their effectiveness. Outposts depend on your book's subject matter and they will be placed where people interested in your subject have a tendency to congregate.

You can find effective outposts in:

a)   Facebook fan page

b)   Photosharing sites, such as photostream on Flickr.com, especially if you have many local places of interest in your novel.

c)   Bookmarking sites like StumbleUpon.com

d) Specialized niche sites like those on Ning.com

87.   You might consider using Apex Reviews to gain a review and develop a video trailer for your book. They charged about $50 for a professional review and a good video. They often run special offers and they are worth a look. With a video, brevity is the key. Keep it short, simple, professional, entertaining and informative.

88. Identify books that are similar to yours and tag your book to it. You will see the tag lines halfway down the Amazon page. Tagging is a great way to bring your book up when readers search a specific genre. Tags can help you find items on Amazon and provide an easy way for you to 'remember' and classify items for later recall.

89.   Make sure that your author biography is available on all your profiles. As an author, you are selling yourself as a product, so it is important to start making the right brand impressions early. Think about whom you know and about your background in terms of how it can help you sell more books.

90. Use the "Tell Your Fans" feature to maximum effect. With the tools built into the fan page, Facebook allows you to import your contacts from Hotmail, Yahoo, etc. This is useful when you're just starting out and want to tell people you already know about your eBook and your growing fan base.

91. Once you have established a fan base, set up a Facebook fan page. This is not essential until you are approaching 5,000 friends but it is worth planning before you reach that level. Promoting your fan page is a campaign in itself so plan a few days to work on it. Put your fan page URL in your email signature. How many emails do you send per day? Now imagine each email you send is a chance for someone new to find out about your awesome fan page! Write a blog post about your new fan page.

Give your readers five compelling reasons why they should join your fan page. Don't beg; just give the reasons why they'll benefit. New fans are going to join and frequent your fan page if they feel they have something to gain by doing so.

92. Tag other, well-trafficked fan pages in your updates. Their fans might see your page and you may get some cross-traffic and cross-promotion.

93. Ask your Twitter followers to join your fan page and follow you on Facebook. Give some convincing reasons why your Tweeters should also join your Facebook community. If Twitter is the new water cooler, think of your fan page as an invite to come in and chat. For example, tweet something like, "Wanting more conversation than 140 characters will allow? Join us on Facebook at http://fb.me/fanpage." A nice and simple request that will get results.

94. Put a fan page widget on your blog or website. You'll be amazed at how many people simply don't know about your fan page. Putting it on your website (i.e. your home base) will get it in front of all of your website visitors.

95. Customize your fan page URL. Vanity URLs are a fantastic way to make your fan page memorable. "Check out this awesome fan page http://facebook.com/awesomefanpage."

96. Put your fan page URL on your business cards, bookmarks and the back cover of your eBook. Combine offline and online promotion by letting the people you meet in real life know about your fan page.

97. Add a link to your fan page on your personal Facebook profile under the 'links' section. This is a "soft sell" of sorts, letting your friends passively know about your page.

98. Ask your fans to kindly post a link to your fan page on their personal profile. As long as you don't ask too often, people tend to be glad to help out. Leverage the power of your existing audience and see the results.

99. Put your fan page URL on your Twitter profile background. Lots of tweeters still use the web-based version and your profile background is a prime piece of web real estate. Cross-media market using one social network to promote another.

100. It may worthwhle joining international websites which can help sell the foreign rights to your book such as IPR Licensing (*www.iprlicensing.co.uk*).

Chapter 9

The Growth and Future for eBooks

The rapid growth of eBooks has largely been driven by problems within the print book industry. Firstly, as authors know all too well, many traditional publishers will not accept non-agented or unsolicited submissions and because agents are oversubscribed and tend to work on a commission-only basis, they generally offer to represent authors with the biggest name each time.

Secondly, book retailers are struggling and printed books are increasingly costly and take a while to arrive, whereas eBooks can be bought for less and downloaded straight away.

Thirdly, the increase of eBooks has driven the growth and reduction in cost of eReaders, which can hold multiple eBooks for you to read, thereby giving you more choice while travelling or on holiday.

Fourthly, eBooks don't require stocking or the prospect of sales returns, so publishers are increasingly publishing new books in digital format to test the market and then printing the most successful ones.

Moreover, eBooks can be produced and published much quicker than print books, and thus can be turned out to meet current demand. For example, when the banking crisis occurred, Mark Leigh wrote and published his humorous *Crash! The Official Bankers Joke Book* within a week.

So, if eBooks provide authors with a direct route to market, are much less costly, can be downloaded immediately, can be easily stored in eReaders and read most anytime, don't require stocking or the risk of returns, can be produced and published within days, and bring a handy residual income, it seems likely that they will continue to increase year on year and take a larger share of the book market.

Still, print book aficionados will say there's nothing like holding a paperback in your hands and it is difficult reading books off the internet or on handheld electronic and mobile devices.

The industry is trying to play catch-up to adapt to the growth in eBooks, to incorporate them into their business models. It's not that traditional publishers will go out of business or that printed books will become obsolete, but the growth of the eBook market will put pressure on retailers to lower their margins and place demands on publishers to capture more of this burgeoning market.

Digitally downloadable books (eBooks) might take over the lion's share of the market and sooner than many may think, as eReaders improve and become more accessible. The key question is will the emergence and growth of eBooks improve the industry and make it less insular and bring quality back to the fore? Let's hope so!

Appendix 1

Book Bloggers

001 Tumbling Books
21st Century Once Upon a Time's
365 Days of Reading
Abibliophobic
Absolute Forest of Words
Absolutely Obsessed
Abundance of Books, An
Actin' Up with Books
Addicted 2 Novels
Addicted To Novels
Adrienne's Book Reviews
Adventures in Biblioland
Adventures of Cecelia Bedelia
After the Last Page
Aine's Realm
AlexEatsBooks
Ali's Bookshelf
Alice in Readerland
Alisia Leavitt
Alisha's World Of Books
Alison Can Read
Along For The Ride
Always Dreaming
Always Lost in Stories
All About the Word Play
All Things Young Adult
All-Consuming Books, Reviews by Tiger

Allure of Books
Almost Grown-up
ALPHA reader
Always YA at Heart
Alyssa's Bookshelf
Amanda's Writings
Amaterasu Reads
Amber's Teen Reads
Ami Blackwelder's Novels
Amusing Mother
Amy Jones Young Adult Fantasy Fiction
An Addicted Book Reader
Anfractuous Bookaholic
Anna Reads
Annie in Wonderland
Annaleese's Book Addiction
Anonymous Reads
Another Book
Another Book Junkie
Angieville
AnimeGirl's Bookshelf
Anxirium
As These Pages Fly
Ashley Loves Books
Ashley Suzanne
Assortments...
Athena's YA Book Reviews
Attack of the Book
Attic, The
Audiobook Angel, The
Aurelia Lit
Aussie Book Shack

Avery's Book Nook
Awesome Bookworm

B.A.M. Book Reviews
Backwards Story, A
Badass Bookie
Baffling, Bonkers, and Brilliant Books!
Banana Pirata
Bart's Bookshelf
Basically Bookworm
Battalion of Words, A
Beastie Books
Beautiful Madness, A
Beauty and the Armageddon
Becky's Barmy Book Blog
Becky's Book Reviews
Been There, Read That
Been There, Read That
Behind A Million And One Pages
BelleBooks
Belle of the Library
Beneath Shining Stars, I Read
Beneath the Moon and Stars
Beneath the Jacket
Between the Bookcovers
Best of YA
Best Way Out is Through, The
Beth Fish Reads
Bethany Book Blog
Bewitched Bookworms
Bewitching Books
Beyond Books

Bibliogrrrl
Bibliophile Brouhaha
Bibliophile Support Group
Bibliophile's Diary, A
Bibliophilia: A Love Story
Bibliophilia - Maggie's Bookshelf
Bibliophilic Book Blog, The
biblioteca reviews
Big Book Little Book Review
Bildungsroman
Bites
Bittersweet Enchantment
Black and Blue Ink
Black Nailed Reviews
Blkosiner's Book Blog
Blog-o-rama
Blog About Nothing, A
[Bloggers [[heart]] Books]
BloggityBLOGS
Bloody Bookaholic
BLT: Books and Literature for Teens
Blythes & Books: Battling Boredom!
Bodacious Pen, The
Boeklover
Book A Day, A
Book Addict
Book Addict PNR
Book Addictions by Christina
Book Angel
Book Angel Booktopia
Book Babe, The
Book Babes, The

Book Basement, The
Book Bind, The
Book Briefs
Book Bubble, The
Book Butterfly, The
Book Buzz, The
Book Cellar, The
BookChewer
Book Chic
Book Chic- In My Mailbox and More
Book Craze
Book Crumbs
Book Diva's Blog
Book 'Em! The Adventures of a Wannabe Librarian
Book Fairy's Haven, The
Book Filled Blog
Book Fly, The
Books for YAs
Book Garden, The
Book Ge3k
Book Geek, The
Book Geek Reviews
Book Girl, The
Book Harbinger
Book Haven
Book Haven Extraordinaire
Book Heist, The
Book Heroine, The
Book Hookup, The
Book In My Hand, The
Book Infinity
Book Journal

Book Junkies
Book Labyrinth
Book Life, The
Book Lungs
Book Memoirs, The
Book Mermaid, The
Book Muncher, The
Book Mystress, The
Book Nerds Across America
Book Nook Girl
Book Nuts Unite
Book Nymph, The
Book Parade
Book Pixie, The
Book Rants
Book Rat, The
Book Reaper
Book Reviews by Reading It All
Book Reviews Centre
Book Sake
Book Scoop, The
Book Scout, The
Book Shop Assistant, The
Book Sisterhood, The
Book Spot, The
Book Stacks On Deck
Book Swarm, The
Book Talk
Book Twirps
Book Upon Book
Book Vacation, A
Book Whales YA book reviews

Book Witch, The
Book Worm Reviews
Book Worms, The
Book Zone (For Boys)
Books4Hearts
Books 4 Teens
BookAHolic Anonymous
Bookaholic Lis
Bookalicious
Bookalicious Ramblings
BookBandit, The
Bookchilla
BookChowDown
Bookette, The
Bookfever
Bookie Monster, The
Bookish
Bookish Blather
Bookish Type, The
Bookishandproud
Booklopedia
BookLover's Diary, A
BookLoversParadise
Bookmarkbelles
Bookmarked
booknook
BookObsessed
bookobsessed84
Bookologist, The
Books: A Love Story
Books: windows on the emotions
Books According to Deb

Books Ahoy

Books and a Cup of Tea

Books And Beyond

Books and Threads

Books are a Girl's Best Friend

Books are Better Than Ice Cream

Books are like People

Books Are Magic

Books Are Vital

Books By Their Cover

Books, College, and Random Things

Books For All Seasons

Books for Bears

Books for Company

Books for Teens

books from a shelf

Books from Bleh to Basically Amazing

Books From Mars

Books Glorious Books

Books In Transit

Books in the Spotlight

Books Like Stars

Books Make Great Lovers

Books of Amanda Land

Books of Amber

Books out the Juaxoo

Books Over Boys

Books, Sweets and Other Treats

Books that Heal Kids

Books That Spark

Books with Bite

Books, books galore

Brooke's Box of Books
Brush Up On Your Reading
Bubble Gum Book Reviews
Bucket List, The
Building a Library
Bumbles and Fairy-Tales
Bundles Of Books
Buried in Books
Buried in Books
Burning.x.Impossibly.x.Bright
Burnt Pages
Busy Bibliophile, The
But What Are They Eating?
Butterfly Feet Walking on Books
By Flashlight

Calcutt Library Happenings
Camisado Mind
Capslock Book Reviews
Captivated Reading
Cari's Book Blog
Carly Reads for TBF!
Casa de Los Nerds
Casual Reader, A
Chachic's Book Nook
Challenging the Bookworm Blog
Chapter by Chapter
Charlotte's Library
Charming Chelsey's
Chasing Empty Pavements
Cheap Reader, The
Cheezyfeet Books

Chey Show, The
ChicaReader
Chick Lit Teens
Chick Loves Lit
Chicklish
Children's War, The
ChooseYA
Christi the Teen Librarian
Christina Reads YA
Cicely Loves Books
Claire Reads
Clean Teen Fiction
Clock Monkey, The
Clover Hill Book Reviews
Coffee Talk
Colleen's Shelf Life
Colorimetry
ComaCalm's Corner
Coming of Age Books
Compulsive Reader, The
Concord Carlisle Young Adult Galley
Confessions of a Bibliovore
Confessions of a Book Addict
Confessions of a Bookaholic
Confessions of a Bookaholic
Confessions of a Readaholic
Consumed by Books
Consumption of Books
Cornucopia of Reviews
Cosy Books
Cotton Candy Reviews
Courtney Reads

Courtney's Book Nook
[Cover to Cover]
Cover to Cover
Cozy Armchair, The
Cozy Reading Corner, The
Cracking the Cover
Crazy Bookworm, The
Crazy Quilts
Creativity's Corner
Crescive Library, The
Critiquing Critica, The
Crooked Shelf, The
Crooked Word, The
crunchings & munchings
CubicleBlindness Book Reviews
Cuddle With This Book
Cup of Tea Reviews
Cupcake and A Latte, A
Curled up with Books
CURLGURL Reads

Daisy Chain Book Reviews
Dahlia's Eclectic Mind
Dana Does Read
Dana's YA Book Pile
Dark-Readers
Darkly Honest
Dawn Kurtagich
Dawn of the Books
Dead Girl Blogs
Dealings of a Book Junkie
Dear Book

Dearest Dreams
Death Books and Tea
Debbie's World of Books
Debz Bookshelf
DeLibarie
DeRaps Reads
Diary of a Bookworm, The
Digesting the Words
DJ's Life in Fiction
Dog-eared and Well-read
Down The Rabbit Hole
Dragons Who Read
Dream of Books, A
Dream Within A Dream, A
Dreaming by Day
Dreaming In The Pages
Dreaming Of Books
Parafantasy
Dystopian Desserts

Eating YA Books
Edifying & Edgy
Electrical Book Cafe, The
Elena's Book Cafe
Elliott Review, The
Eleusinian Mysteries
Emilie's Book World
Emily Reads (A Lot!)
Emily's Reading Room
Empire of Books
Ems Book Nook
Ending Unplanned

Entre Libros
Epic Book Nerd
Epilogue
Escape Through the Pages
Escape to Wonderland
Escapism Project
Esther's Ever After
Evergreen Junior High Library
Everlasting Enchantments
Everything to do with Books
Excellent Reads
Ezine of A Random Girl

Fabbity Fab Book Reviews
Fable Faerie, The
Fabulous Gift of Life, The
Faery Tale Addict
Fairytale Nerd, The
Fall Into Books
Falling For Books
Fanatics Book Blog, A
Fans of Fiction
Fantastic Book Review
Fantastic Finds
Fantasy's Ink
Fantasy4eva
Fay-Bay's Books
FICBookReviews
Fiction Fairy, The
Fiction Fascination
Fiction Folio
Fiction Spark

Fresh Dawgs' Book Blog
Friend With Chocolate, A
From a Book Lover
From The Bookshelf of T.B.
From Y to A

GalleySmith
Gardening Literature
Geek Girl's Book Blog
Geeks & Books
Geeky Beach Babe, The
Geeky Reads
Getting Lost in Words
Gilbert & Gomez
GingerRead Reviews
Girl About Books
girl loves books
Girls In The Stacks.com
Girls Without a Bookshelf
Glass of Wine, A
Glitter Lit
Gripped Into Books
Gobs and Gobs of Books
Goddess Librarian
Good Book and the Random Movie
Good Books For Kids
Good Addiction, A
Good Golly Miss Molly
Grammarian's Reviews, The
Graveyard Library, The
GReads!
Great Raven, The

Green Bean Teen Queen
GreenLillipads
Growing Up YA
Guy Gone Geek

Habermann Press, The
Hampton Reviews
Handle Like Hendrix
Happy Nappy Bookseller, The
Hardcover Harlequin, The
Harley Bear Book Blog
Harmony Book Reviews
Harmony's Radiant Reads
Haunting of Orchid Forsythia, The
Heart Of Dreams, The
Heaven, Hell and Purgatory Book Reviews
Heaven is a Bookstore
He Followed Me Home... Can I Keep Him?
Heise Reads & Recommends
Helen's Book Blog
Her Stardust Soul
Here's to Us
Hey Read This Book
Hey, Teenager of the Year
Hidden Adventures of a Teenage Reader
Hiding in the Stacks
Hiding Spot, The
Hippies, Beauty, and Books. OH MY!
Hobbitsies
Holes in My Brain
Hooked on Books

Hooked to Books
Hope, Faith & Books
Hope, Love, and Happy Endings
How I see it

I Blog, You Read
I Eat Words
I Heart Books
I Heart Monster
I Heart YA Books
I Just Wanna Sit Here and Read
I Like These Books
I Live in a Fictional World
I Read Banned Books
I Read to Relax!
I Read Therefore I Am
I Swim for Oceans
I Want to Read That
I Was a Teenage Book Geek
I Write, I Read, I Review
Ian's Realm and More
IB Book Blogging
IB Teen Blog
Icey Books
Icy Sweetness
I'd So Rather Be Reading
If You Liked That...
iLive, iLaugh, iLove Books
I'm Loving Books - YA Paranormal Book Reviews
Imaginary Reads
Imaginative Adventure: A Young Adult Book Blog
Improbable Fiction, An

In Bed with Books
In Between the Lines
In Between the Pages
In Between Writing and Reading
In Interest
In the Best Worlds
In the Closet with a Bibliophile
In The Good Books
In Which a Girl Reads
Independent Reads
IndigoHues
Infinite Booklist, The
Ink, Paper & Imagination
Ink Puddle, The
Ink Scratchers
Inked Books
Inked ON
Inklings Read.
Inside the Mind
Into The Morning Reads
Into the Wardrobe
iRead!
Irish Banana Review, The
Irresistible Rea ds
Ivan Bookworm
Ivy's Reads

J'adore Happy Endings
Jagged Edge Reviews
Jelly Loves Books
jennreadsfiction
Jessica's Bookshelf

Jillicious Reading
JJ iReads
Juiciliciousss Reviews
Jump Into Books
Juniper Breeze is Blowing In, The
Just a Book Crazy, Jane Austen Lovin' Gal
Just a Booklover
Just Another Teenage Bookworm
Just Bookin' Around
Just Blinded Book Reviews
Just One More Chapter
Just Read
Just Your Typical Book Blog
Justin's Book Blog

Kaitlyn in Bookland
karenschoice-books
Karin's Book Nook
Karla Reads
Kate Hinderer Writes
Kate's Tales of Books and Bands
Katelyn's Blog
Katherine Was Thinking
Kathy's Library
Katie's Book Blog
kayla THE bookworm
Keep Calm and Kari On
KelseyAnne's Book Blog
Kid Lit Reviews
Kindle and Me
KindleObsessed
Kindling the Fire

Kindred Dreamheart
Kitty Korner Library
Kitty's Bookshelf

La Femme Readers
Lady Reader's Bookstuff
Lady Scribble's Book Blog
Laina Has Too Much Spare Time
Larkin's Book Bloggers
Last Word, The
Late Bloomer Online
Lateiner Gang Book Review Spot
Laura's Review Bookshelf
Lauren's Crammed Bookshelf
Lauren Gets Literal
LC's Adventures in Libraryland
Le' Grande Codex
Le Petit Book Reviews
Le Vanity Victorienne
Leah's YA Bookshelf
Leitora, A
LeseLust & LeseLiebe
Letras y Escenas'
Letters Inside Out
Libraries and Young Adults
Librarian Reads, The
Library in the Tower, The
Library Lurker, The
Librarykat's World
Libri Dilectio
LibriCritic
Libros con alma

Life After Jane
Life After Twilight
Life of Fiction, The
Life of Literature, A
Lil Red's Hood
Lilly Road (YA)
LindsayWrites
Linny's Literature
Literary Life
Literary Exploration
Literary Obsession
Literature for Lunch
Little Book Blog, The
Little Book Owl
Little Bookworm, The
Little Library Muse
Little Shelf of Heaven, A
Little Squeed
Livin' Life Through Books
Living, Loving, Laughing, Reading
LiyanaLand!
Locket Stories
Logan E. Turner
Looksie Lovitz: Books and Wits
Loony-Reads
Lost Amongst the Shelves
Lost in Stories
Lost in Y.A. Wonderland
Lost in a YA Book
Lost in the Library
Lost in the Pages
Loud Words & Sounds

Love.Book.Addict
Love The Way You Read
Love YA Lit
Lovely Getaway, The
Lovely Lil' Book Worm
Lovely Little Book Blog, A
Lover of Paranormal and Indies
Loves to Read
LoveReadingX
Lucid Conspiracy

Madame Bookworm
Maestra Amanda's Bookshelf
Magic Attic, The
Magic Attic Reviews, The
Magic Bean Review
Magical Books
Mairi's Library
Makeshift Bookmark
Making the Grade: YA Lit Reviews
Manda's Movements
Manga Maniac Cafe
Manhattan Reader
Maniacal Bookworm, The
marie LOVES books
Marjolein's Book Blog
Mary Read A Lot (A Book A Day)
Maw Books Blog
мαувє ιtz ℓσvє
Me and the Bookshelf Life
Melissa's Bookshelf

MemoriesOvertakingMe
Mera's YA Book List
Merlin, YA Books, and More
Mermaid Vision Books
Michelle and Leslie's Book Picks
Michelle's Bookshelf
Midnight Bloom Reads
Midnight Bookworm, The
Midnight Fantasies
Midnight Garden, The : YA Books for Adults
Midnight Glance
Midnight Reader
Midnight Reads
Mile Long Bookshelf, The
Mimi Valentine
Mimosa Stimulus, The
Mind Reading?
Mindful Musings Book Blog
Mint Tea and A Good Book
Mirrorcle World
Miss Bookiverse
Miss Page-Turner's City of Books
Miss Print
Miss Remmers' Review
Mission to Read
Missy's Reads & Reviews
Mixtures: Books...+
Mod Podge Bookshelf, The
Mode A La Pie
Moirae (the fates)
Mom Reads My Books!
Mon Palais

Monster of Books
Moody Teenager, The
Moonlight Book Reviews
Moonlight Gleam's Bookshelf
More Than Just A Book
Mortal's Library, The
Most Important Letter
Mostly Reading YA
Mountains of Instead, The
Mr. Book Wonder
Mr. Ripleys Enchanted Books
Mrs. Boswell's Book Bag
Mrs. Librarian Lady
Mrs.ReaderPants
Mrs. K's Bookshelf
Mrs. V's Reviews
Ms Book Queen
Much Loved Books
Mug of Moxie
Muggle-Born
Mulberry St. Blog, The
Mundie Moms
Musings of a Reader Happy
Musing of a YA Reader
Must Love Books
Must Read Faster
My Book Diaries
My Book Journey
My Favourite Books
My Girl Friday
My Head is Full of Books
My Home Away From Home

My Luv 4 YA Books
My Not So Vacant Shelf
My Overstuffed Bookshelf
My Pile Of Books
My Reading Frenzy
My Summer Girl Books
My Words Ate Me
Myriad of Books, A
Mystical Lit. Lounge

Nap. Snack. Read. Three essentials for life.
Narratively Speaking
Narrowing Road, The
Natalie and the Ever-Growing Bookshelf
Natsgoldenbooks
Naughty Book Kitties, The
Nawanda Files
Nazish Reads
Nerd Girl Reads & Writes
Nerds Wife, The
Neverending Fantasy, A
Neverending Shelf, The
New Kind of Ordinary, A
Nick's Book Blog
Nicole Passante
Nicole's Library
Nicoleslaw00 Book Blog
Night Bookmobile, The
Night Life, The
Night's Dream of Books, A
Niki's Book Reviews
Ninja Librarian

Nobody Knows
Nom Nom Tasty Books
Nook of Books
Not Another Book Blog
Not Enough Bookshelves
Not-so-young-adult Librarian
Not Your Fairy Tale
Novapsych
Novel Affair, The
Novel Novice
Novel Minded
Novel Nerd, The
Novel Nerds
Novel Nymph, The
Novel Paradise, A
Novel Society
Novel Sounds
Novel Thoughts
Noveladay
Novels on the Run

O'Boyled Books
Obsessions Of A Bookaholic
OCD about Books
Of Wonder and Dreams
Off My Bookshelf
Off The Shelf
Oh, For the Love of Books!
On Emily's Bookshelf
On The Nightstand
On The Shelf
Once Upon a Bookcase

Precious, My
Presenting Lenore
Pretty Books
Pretty in Fiction
Pretty Nifty (YA) Reader
Princess Bookie
Princess Pandoryss
Pure Imagination
Pure Textuality

QT Book Worm
Queen of Teen Fiction, The
QueerYA
Quinn's Book Nook
Quirky Fate Press

Rachel Reads
Radiant Shadows
Raindrop Reflections
Rajiv's Reviews
Rambling Bookmarks
Rambling of a Book Nerd
Rambling Reader
Ramblings Of a Teenage Bookworm
Random Chalk Talk
Random Girl Book Blog
Random Reading Rants and Reviews
Rants N Scribbles
Rants, Writings, & Reviews of the Forever Young, The
Raving Reviewer
Re-Shelf, The
Read Between the Lines

Read It, See It
Read Me, Bookmark Me, Love Me
Read 'n' Write
Read Now Sleep Later
Read This Book
Read What You Know
Read. Watch. Listen
Read. Write. Ramble.
readaholicme
Readaraptor
Reader Bee, The
Reader Girls, The
Reader with a Voice
Reader's Adventure, A
Reader's Heartstring, The
Reader's Pensieve, A
Readers and Whiners
Readers GUYde, The
Readers Haven
Readers Unite
Reading A Little Bit Of Everything
Reading Addict
Reading Angel
Reading Away The Days!
Reading Between Classes
Reading by Moonlight
Reading Cause I'm Addicted
Reading Date, The
Reading Daydreamer, A
Reading Fever, The
Reading Geek, The
Reading Girl (: , The

Reading in Color
Reading in the Corner
Reading is Bliss
Reading is Endless
Reading Obsession
Reading or Breathing
Reading Princess
Reading Rants! Out of the Ordinary Teen Booklist!
Reading Rocks
Reading Stands Forever
Reading Teen
Reading the Best of the Best
Reading Underground
Reading Vacation
Reading Wishes
Reading with ABC
Reading, Writing, and Waiting
Reading Writing Breathing Book Reviews
Reading Zombies
Reading@Berkeley High
Readingjunky's Reading Roost
Readings of Benji
Readinista
Reads With Wreckless Abandon
Readventurer, The
Realm of Fiction
Rebecca-Books
Reclusive Bibliophile
Redhead Heroines
Reed Reads Book Reviews
Refracted Light | Young Adult Book Reviews
Relook the Book

Scribble by Moonlight
Scribbler in the Rye, The
Scribing Shadows
Secret Book Lover, The
Secret Life of an Avid Reader, The
Secret Life of a Bibliophile, The
Sea of Pages, A
SeeitORreadit
See Michelle Read
Serendipity
Serene Hours
Serpentine Library, The
Shadow Kisses Book Reviews
Shady Glade, The
Shae Carcar
Sharon Loves Books and Cats
Shelf Conscious Books
ShhMommysReading
Shiirleyy's Bookshelf
Short and Sweet
Shooting Stars Mag
Shut Up! I'm Reading
Simply Books
Sincerely, A Reader
Singing and Reading in the Rain
SisterSpooky: Book Fangirl
Sizzling Reads
skoobdoog
Small Review
Snowdrop Dreams of Books
So Many Books, So Little Time
So Many Books, So Little Time

Storybook Escape
Storybound Girl
Straight From the Writer's Mouth
Strawberry Splash Book Reviews
Subtle Chronicler, The
Such A Teenage Bookworm
Summer Books
Super Reader Girl's Book Reviews
Supercalifragilciiousreads
Supernatural Bookworm
Supernatural Snark
Surreal & Sublime
Svarstymas Reviews
Sweet Bookshelf, The
Sweety Readers
Swords for Fighting

Tabithas' Book Blog
Tale of Many Reviews, A
Tales Compendium, The
Tales of a Ravenous Reader
Tales of a Teenage Bookaholic
Tales of a Teenage Book Lover
Tale of Many Reviews, A
Tapestry of Words, A
Tantalizing Illusions
Tarah Dunn
Tater's Tall Tails
Tattooed Books
Tay's Bookshelf
Tea Mouse
Teach 8 YA Book Blog

Teen Bibliophile, The
Teen Book Fanatics
Teen Book Guru, The
Teen Bookworm, The
Teen Girl Reads
Teen Librarian's Toolbox
Teen Reader Queen, The
Teen Readers' Diary
Teen-sy Little Book Blog
TeenageReader
Teens Know Best!
Teens Read?
Teens Read and Write
Teen Text Talk
TeenyReader
Ten Cent Notes
That Book Blog
That Bookish Girl
That Cover Girl
That Hapa Chick
That's Swell
{the} book/
The Here. The Now. And the Books!
There's A Book
This Blonde Reads
{This Girl Reads}
This Purple Crayon
ThirstforFiction
Thoughts of a Book Junky, The
Three Rivers Library Teens
Through the Looking Glass
Through the Wardrobe

Urban Fantasy Land

Vampyre Gurls Book Club
Verb Vixen
Verbose Vegetarian, The
Vicky's Volumes
Views & Reviews
Vintage Bookworm, The
Violet Hour, The
vvb32 reads
Vy's Blog

Wandering Fangirl, The
Want My YA
Watercolor Moods
We Fancy Books
We Heart YA
Welcome to my life...
Well-Read Reviews
What Bri Reads
What I Read Yesterday
What Miss Kelley Is Reading
What Mrs. Light is Reading
What To Read. What To Read.
What YA Reading?
Whatever You Can Still Betray
What's Beyond Forks?
What's Your Story?
whatchYAreadin?
Where You Go From Here
wherethewildbooksare
Whimsical Fic-ery

whnbstihwsoft
Why I YA
Wicked Awesome Books
Wildly Read
Willa's Ramblings
With A Book
Within Pages
Windowpane Memoirs
Wisdom From A Teenage Bookworm
Wolf's Den, The
Wonderful World of Word, The
Wondrous Reads
Wood's Books
Word for Teens
Word Girl
Word Nerd, The
Words Like Silver
Words and Whispers
Words on Paper
Words That Fly
Words World and Wings
Words on the Shelf
World, My
World of Words, A
Worn Pages and Dusty Shelves
WovenStrands
Write for a Reader
Write Obsession, The
Writing From the Tub
Writing Wonderland, The
Written Rhapsody, A
Written World, The

Writtled
Wyz Reads

Xpresso Reads
xo'reads

YA Addict
YA Between the Lines
YA Bibliophile
YA Bliss

YA Book Nerd
YA Book Nuts
YA Book Queen
YA Book Reads
YA Book Reviews
YA Book Seasons
YA Book Shelf
YA Book Shelf, The
YA Bookcase on Lake Street, The
YA Bookie Monster
YA Booklover Blog
YA Bookmark
YA Books
YA Books and More
Y.A Bookworm, The
Y.A. Bookworm Blogger , The
YA Bound
YA Café, The
YA Crush
YA Fantasy Guide
YA Fiction Freaks

YA Highway
YA Infatuation
YA Librarian Tales
YA Lit Crave
YA Lit in 100 Words or Less
YA Litwit
Y.A. Love
YA Magic Pages
YA Overindulgence
YA Reader, The
YA Reads
YA Sweet Escape
YA Urban
YA-Sisterhood
YA, YA, YAs, The
YA Yeah Yeah
YA? Y Not?
YA2BOK
YAkety YAks
YAL Book Briefs
YAthenaeum
Yay! Reads
You Know What They Say About Book People?
Young Adult 4 Life
Young Adult (& Kids) Books Central Blog
Young Adult Book Haven
Young Adult Book Reviews
Young Adult Book Reviews by Liz Winn
Young Adult Books You'll Love :)
Young Adult Connection, The
Young Adult Critic
Young Adult Fiction Today

Young Adult Literature Lover
Young Adult Novel Reader
Young Readers
You Know You Want to Read It
You're Killing Me

Zealous Reader, The
Zoe's Book Reviews
Zoey's Uncreatively Titled Blog
Zone Out Mode

Appendix 2

Book Reviewers

The Bloomsbury Review
Attn: Ray Gonzalez
1553 Platte Street, Ste. 206
Denver, CO 80202-1167
303-455-3123
e-mail: bloomsb@aol.com

Booklist
American Library Association
Attn: Brad Hooper
50 East Huron Street
Chicago, IL 60611
Tel: 312-280-5757
e-mail: bhooper@ala.org

Library Journal
Attn: Book Room
249 W. 17th Street
New York, NY 10011
Tel: 212-463-6819

East Bay Express
Stephen Buell
1335 Stanford Avenue, Ste. 100
Emeryville, CA 94608
510-879-3700

Marin Independent Journal
Vicky Larson, Lifestyles Editor
P.O. Box 6150
Novato, CA 94948
415-883-8600

The New York Times Book Review
Editor
620 Eighth Avenue
New York, NY 10018
books@nytimes.com

San Francisco Chronicle Book Review
John McMurtrie, Editor
901 Mission Street
San Francisco, CA 94119-2988

The Village Voice
Brian Parks
36 Cooper Square
New York, NY 10003

San Francisco Magazine
243 Vallejo Street
San Francisco, CA 94111
Articles Editor: Nina Martin
Reviews Editor: Mia Lipman
415-398-2800

American Book Reviewers
Rebecca Kaiser, Managing Editor
Illinois State University
Campus Box No. 4241
Normal, IL 61790-4241

The Believer Book Review
185 Claremont Avenue, 6K
New York, NY 10027
believermag.org

The Carolina Quarterly
Tessa Joseph

CB 3520, Greenlaw Hall
UNC-Chapel Hill
Chapel Hill, NC 27599

The Chattahoochee Review
Marc Fitten
Georgia Perimeter College
2101 Womack Rd.
Dunwoody, GA 30338-4497

Connecticut Review
Dr. Vivian Shipley
Southern Community State University
501 Crescent Street
New Haven, CT 06473

Del Sol Review
Michael Neff
2020 Pennsylvania Avenue, NW
Washington, DC 20006

Foreword
Alex Moore
129 1/2 East Front Street
Traverse City, MI 94684

The Georgia Review
Stephen Corey
University of Georgia
Athens, GA 30602-9009

The Gettysburg Review
Peter Stitt
Gettysburg College
Gettysburg, PA 17325-1491

The Iowa Review
David Hamilton
308 EPB
University of Iowa
Iowa City, IA 52242

Kenyon Review
David Baker
Finn House
102 Wiggin Street
Kenyon College
Gambier, OH 433022-9623

The Marlboro Review
Ellen Dudley
PO Box 243
Marlboro, VT 05344

New England Review
C. Dale Young
Middlebury College
Middlebury, VT 05753

New Letters Magazine
Robert Stewart, Editor
University House
5101 Rockhill Road
Kansas City, MO 64110

North Dakota Quarterly
Donald Junkins
University of North Dakota
Grand Forks, ND 58202-7209
Chicago, IL 60614

Prairie Schooner

Hilda Raz
University of Nebraska
Lincoln, NE 68588-0334

Salamander
Jennifer Barber
Suffolk University/English Department
41 Temple Street
Boston, MA 02113-4280

The Sewanee Review
Bob Jones, Editor
735 University Avenue
Sewanee, TN 37383

Shenandoah
R. T. Smith, Editor
Mattingly House, 2 Lee Avenue
Washington and Lee University
Lexington, VA 24450-2116

Southern Humanities Review
Virginia Kouidis
9088 Haley Center
Auburn, AL 36849-5202

The Southern Review
Jeanne Leiby
Old President's House
Louisiana State University
Baton Rouge LA 70803

TriQuarterly
Susan Firestone Hahn
629 Noyes Street
Evanston, IL 60208

The Virginia Quarterly Review
Ted Genoways
One West Range
PO Box 400223
Charlottesville, VA 22904-4223

Wind
Rebecca Howell, Editor
P.O. Box 24548
Lexington, KY 40524

Women's Review of Books
Amy Hoffman
Centers for Women CHE
Wellesley College
106 Central Street
Wellesley, MA 02181

Zone 3
Susan Wallace, Managing Editor
P.O. Box 4265
APSU
Clarksville, TN 37044

The Writers Chronicle
Associated Writing Programs
Tallwood House, Mail Stop 1E3
George Mason University
Fairfax, VA 22030

Crossroads
Christina Davis, Editor
Poetry Society of America
15 Gramercy Park
New York, NY 10003

National Book Critics Circle includes:

Eric Banks, NBCC
57 Grand Street, Apt. 4
Brooklyn, NY 11211

Jane Ciabattari, NBCC
36 West 75th Street, 5A
New York, NY 10023

Rigoberto Gonzálezm NBCC
104-60 Queens Blvd #8-R
Forest Hills, NY 11375

Mary Ann Gwinn, NBCC
P.O. Box 70
Seattle, WA 98111

Barbara Hoffert, NBCC
360 Park Avenue South
New York, NY 10010

Steven G. Kellman, NBCC
302 Fawn Drive
San Antonio, TX
78231-1519

Karen Long, NBCC
3114 Berkshire Rd.
Cleveland Heights, OH 44118

James Marcus, NBCC
345 East 52nd Street, Apt 10E
New York, NY 10022

Maureen N. McLane, NBCC

New York University
Department of English
13 University Place, Room 528
New York, NY 10003

Scott McLemee, NBCC
1711 Mass Ave, NW, #321
Washington, DC 20036

Laurie Muchnickm NBCC
731 Lexington Avenue
New York, NY 10022

Kevin Prufer, NBCC
305 Zoll Street
Warrensburg, MO 64093

John Reed, NBCC
c/o Baby Rock
22 Howard Street #3J
New York, NY 10013

Jennifer Reese, NBCC
2 Carolyn Lane
Mill Valley, CA 94941

Carlin Romano
Geeta Sharma-Jensen, NBCC
333 W. State Street
Milwaukee, WI 53203

Lizzie Skurnick, NBCC
296 Marlboro Road
Englewood, NJ 07631

Elizabeth Taylor, NBCC

435 N. Michigan Ave.
Chicago, IL 60611

Craig Morgan Teicher
Publishers Weekly/NBCC
360 Park Avenue South
New York, NY

David L. Ulin, NBCC
1089 South Genesee Ave
Los Angeles, CA 90019

Oscar Villalon
3643 25th St.
San Francisco, CA 94110

Eric Miles Williamson, NBCC
3913 Martin Avenue
McAllen, TX 78504

Art Winslow, NBCC
39 Point Street
New Hamburg, NY 12590

Linda Wolfe, NBCC
247 W. 87th St. Apt. 5J
New York, NY 10024

Council of Literary Magazines and Presses
154 Christopher Street, Suite 3C
New York, NY 10014-2839

BookSense.com
Linda M. Castellitto, Creative Director
828 S. Broadway
Tarrytown, NY 10591

tel: 914-591-2665. ext. 1235
fax: 914-591-2710
e-mail: linda@booksense.com

Education Digest
Pam Moore, Managing Editor
P.O. Box 8623
Ann Arbor, MI 481
www.edigest.com

NewPages
P.O. Box 1580
Bay City, MI 48706
www.newpages.com/bookreviews

Rain Taxi
P.O. Box 3840
Minneapolis, MN 55403
www.raintaxi.com

The "Constant Critic"
www.constantcritic.com

100 Top Tips for Selling eBooks in this book

Summary Checklist

1. Write hooks into your eBook

2. Mention places in your book to reach pockets of interest

3. Build reader loyalty by subtly mentioning fans, friends & family in your eBook

4. Keep your vocabulary simple and concise

5. Hit the ground running with an exciting first line, first paragraph and first chapter

6. Keep the story flowing and don't be over-descriptive

7. Use an eBook template for formatting and add a 'Look Inside' feature

8. Reflect the genre and content in book title

9. Judge your book by its cover

10. Write catchy synopsis & add endorsements to back cover

11. Create an interesting preview

12. Build a relationship with your readers

13. Choose your digital platform carefully

14. Sell through multiple eBookstores and list your book in directories

15. Create sales page optimized for search engines

16. Make book available in multiple file formats

17. Use E-Junkie for eBook delivery & affiliates

18. Price your book intelligently

19. Avoid under-pricing your book

20. Set low price point for your first book

21. Experiment on pricing & monitor closely

22. Charge what you would pay for book

23. Base pricing on quality, not book length

24. Keep a checklist of promotional activity

25. Avoid engaging companies to draft or distribute press releases for you

26. Seek out third-party endorsements

27. Build your profession into your Facebook page

28. Build your profile positively

29. Join relevant online groups

30. Update & inform readers about your books

31. Increase friends/contacts & set up an event

32. Keep your author page fun & interesting

33. Your Twitter username should include author or writer in it

34. Use Twitterific

35. Search out relevant contacts in book world

36. Search for eBook review groups & eBook retweeting groups

37. Keep an eye on followers daily

38. Tweet useful links & ideas

39. Pick up followers with useful content

40. Retweet followers to build brand loyalty

41. Build trust with your tweets

42. Familiarize yourself with postings links & photographs

43. Join LinkedIn

44. Join marketing groups & book forums

45. Link LinkedIn account to Twitter account

46. Join MySpace, Ning, Bebo & video-sharing sites

47. Create Facebook & Twitter account for your eBook protagonist

48. Join social networks such as Plaxo, Ryze & BranchOut

49. Join social bookmarking sites like Shelfari, weRead & use MeetUp

50. Use Clickbank & Tradebit for your affiliate programs

51. Avoid spending money on pay-per-click traffic generators

52. Write a blog & keep it current

53. Ensure your promotion is as professional as your book

54. Seek reviews & reply to all of them

55. Offer limited period discounts & create bundles

56. Build a loyal readership

57. Offer 1st chapter for free on Mass-EBooks

58. Search local directories for relevant links

59. Contact local press for feature article or review

60. Write personalized letters to local venues

61. Tailor presentations to book writing rather than storyline

62. Seek out regional associations you have links with

63. Contact writing groups

64. Contact local and regional libraries

65. Leave a gift & never ask to be paid

66. Ensure promotional materials are current

67. Leave your Facebook & Twitter details

68. Monitor sales closely

69. Set reachable & measurable goals

70. Print some sample books on Lulu.com or Createspace

71. Develop author website to showcase your writing in general and eBook in particular

72. Inform your readers regularly of progress

73. Keep press/media outlets updated

74. Make press releases professional & interesting

75. Create a press kit

76. Organize radio interviews

77. Temper any direct marketing

78. Keep in regular contact with your readers

79. Practice & polish your presentations

80. Enter your eBook into literary competitions

81. Attend literary festivals & book fairs

82. Enlist your friends & family

83. Join Goodreads.com

84. Join Kindleboards.com

85. Adapt your eBook to other markets & formats

86. Set up Outposts

87. Consider using Apex Reviews

88. Tag your eBook to similar books

89. Add your author bio to all your profiles

90. Use "Tell Your Fans" feature to full effect

91. Set up Facebook fan page

92. Tag well-trafficked fan pages

93. Ask Twitter followers to join your fan page

94. Put fan page widget on your blog or website

95. Customize your fan page URL

96. Put fan page on all promotional literature

97. Link to fan page on your Facebook profile

98. Ask fans to post a link on their profile

99. Put your fan page URL on your Twitter profile background

100. Add your book to IPR Licensing

Glossary of Terms

Affiliate Marketing: Performance-based marketing in which other sites are rewarded for each visitor or customer brought about by its own marketing effort.

Amazon.com: The leading online retailer of books in the world today.

Author Brand: How much your books are recognized and how well you are known as a published author.

Author Platform: How well-positioned you are to sell and market your book, including your readership/fan base, availability/visibility and authority to help your book reach its intended target audience.

Bebo.com: An acronym for "Blog Early, Blog Often". Bebo is a social networking site that has a section dedicated to writers called *Bebo Authors*.

*Blog (*short for *Web log)*: Online journal updated regularly and reflecting the author's interests and current activities.

BranchOut: Facebook.com application designed for networking professionally.

Calibre-eBook.com: A free and open source e-book library management application.

Clickbank: The Internet's leading retailer of digital products including eBooks.

Digital Download: The process of copying an eBook to a computer or eReader (ie. handheld devices like Nook and Kindle).

Direct Marketing: Sending and selling your book directly to readers and retailers, typically through e-mail, telephone, post or fax.

eBook: A book-length publication in digital format, consisting of text, images, or both, and produced on, published through, and readable on computers or other electronic devices.

E-Commerce: Online selling, typically involving the acceptance of credit card details, site security for online transactions, and an order fulfilment process in place.

E-Junkie.com: A copy & paste, hosted shopping cart and digital delivery service which includes eBooks.

eReader (electronic reader): Hand-held device such as Kindle, iPad, Nook, iPhone, Sony Reader and Kobo to download and read eBooks.

e-tailer: Online retailer like Amazon and Barnes & Noble for listing and selling eBooks.

Facebook.com: Social networking website on which you can add friends to your Facebook page and send them messages, alerting them about new events in your life, such as the publication of your eBook.

Fan page: A facility on Facebook that enables you to build up a following for your eBook by sending regular updates to an unlimited number of people, and keep the focus on the organization without revealing the administrator (unless you want to).

Flickr.com: An image hosting and video hosting website, web services suite, and online community.

Gather.com: A social networking website designed to encourage interaction through various social, political and cultural topics.

Goodreads.com: A privately-run social cataloguing website which permits individuals to sign up and register books to create their library catalogues and reading lists. It also allows users to create their own groups of book suggestions and discussion topics.

Google adwords: Pay-per-click advertising and site-targeted advertising for text, banner, and rich-media ads.

Guerrilla Marketing: An unconventional way of performing promotional activities on a low budget, relying more on time, energy and imagination than a big marketing spend.

Hooks in books: A narrative inclusion that captures the reader's interest, eg. by including recognizable character and place names.

IPRLicensing.co.uk: An international rights website which enables authors to list and sell the rights for their eBook to the world via a global network.

Kindle: The world's best-selling handheld e-Reader (eBook reading device).

Kindleboards: Forum and discussion group facility available on Kindle to discuss and promote eBooks.

Kobobooks.com: Major online retailer of eBooks. *Kobo e-Readers* are handheld eBook reading devices.

LinkedIn.com: Social networking website for people in professional occupations, such as publishing.

Look Inside!: A free facility offered by Amazon for you to show sample pages of your eBook to entice readers to buy your book.

Lovereading.com: The largest UK book club on the internet along with its partner site, Lovewriting.com, offering advice on publishing your work, and making it easy for people to sample, review and purchase your eBook.

Marketing Campaign: The activities you undertake to raise your literary profile as a published author and promote and sell copies of your book.

Mass-Ebooks.com: A website offering free eBook downloads.

Media Kit / Press Pack: A collection of marketing materials including a press release, author brief, fact sheet about your book, current news, suggested interview Q & As and your contact details which can be sent to the media to publicize your book.

Ning.com: A social networking site enabling you to create your own social networking site based on a particular subject, such as your eBook.

Nook: Hand-held electronic book reader developed by American book retailer Barnes & Noble.

Offline Marketing: Traditional methods of marketing such as television/newspaper/magazine adverts, billboards, posters, jingles, etc.

Online Marketing (*webvertising* or *e-marketing*): The promotion of products like eBooks over the internet through search engine marketing and optimization, social media, affiliate marketing, pay-per-click and banner ads, and e-mail marketing.

Outposts: Developing your social media postings to help attract your target audience and build brand recognition for your eBooks.

Paypal.com: A global e-commerce business allowing payments and money transfers to be made through the Internet. Online money transfers serve as electronic alternatives to paying with traditional paper methods, such as checks and money orders.

Pay-per-click (PPC) advertising: A form of online marketing where you bid on specific key words and key word phrases relevant to your website or eBook so when someone puts those words into an internet search engine, banners and links are provided to your website. Each time someone clicks on these banners or links and are directed to your website, you pay a small fee to the PPC advertiser.

Plaxo.com: An online address book and social networking service.

Podcasting: Recording videos and making them available on the internet to anyone with a speedy internet connection.

Press Release: Short (typically one or two pages) announcement of newsworthy events associated with your book.

PR websites / Newswires: Distributors for press releases on the internet.

Publishing Platform (for eBooks): An e-publishing platform that allows the management of content, the definition of digital rights, authentication scenarios, the management of customers and e-commerce transactions, and the incorporation of marketing tools and text retrieval.

Reciprocal links: A mutually-agreed link between your website and another site intended to increase the numbers of visitors to both sites, and thereby achieve higher ranking on search engines, giving your site more prominence and (hopefully) your eBook more sales.

Ryze.com: Free social networking website designed to link business professionals and entrepreneurs.

Scribd.com: A digital documents library that allows users to publish, discover, share and discuss original writings in various languages. Allows users to post documents in various formats and embed them into a web page.

Search Engine Optimization: Tailoring your website so when people search online for subjects related to your book on various browsers such like Google and Yahoo, they might find and access your website.

Shelfari.com: A social cataloguing website for books. Users build virtual bookshelves of titles they own or have read and can rate, review, tag, discuss and recommend books to others.

Smashwords.com: A DIY eBook self-publishing and distribution platform.

Social Bookmarking: A service on the internet for storing, sharing and discovering popular content. Instead of saving website links to your web browser, you save them to the web. Because your bookmarks are online, you can easily share them with friends.

Social Media: Web- and mobile-based technologies to turn communication into interactive dialogue among organizations, communities, and individuals. This includes internet forums, weblogs, social blogs, micro-blogging, wikis, social networks, podcasts and social bookmarking.

Social Networking: Expanding your contacts by making connections through attending events and meeting individuals. On the internet, establishing interconnected communities (commonly known as personal networks) that help people make contacts that would be good for them to know.

Target Market: A group of people identified as those most likely to buy your book.

Thumbnail: Reduced-size versions of pictures, used to help in recognizing and organizing them.

Tradebit.com: Offers bandwidth / traffic to anybody who wants to sell eBook downloads and files online (with PayPal, Google Checkout or Clickbank).

Twitter.com: A free web-based service enabling its users to send and read text-based messages of up to 140 characters, known as *tweets*.

Typepad: Online service for hosting and publishing weblogs and photo albums, and supports a LinkedIn application that pulls blog posts into LinkedIn.

URL (uniform research locator)/Domain Name:
The internet address for your website, generally beginning with http://www or simply www. and ending with .com, .co.uk, .net., .org, and so on.

Video blogging (vlogging or vidblogging): A form of blogging where short videos are made regularly and often combines embedded video or a video link with supporting text, images, and other data.

Viral Marketing: Increasing awareness of you as a published author and your eBook through people talking about your eBook and recommending it to others.

WeRead.com: A popular online community of book enthusiasts.

Word-of-Mouse Marketing: Using social media sites on the internet to create a buzz about your eBook.

Word-of-Mouth Marketing (see - Viral Marketing): Speaking with people and groups of people directly to create a following for your book.

Wordpress.com: A free and open source blogging tool.

YouTube: A video-sharing website on which users can upload, share and view videos, enabling authors to showcase themselves and their books.

Zinepal.com: Enables authors to create eBooks from online content or read eBooks created by others.